D1570204

NEVADA

MYTHS & LEGENDS

THE TRUE STORIES BEHIND HISTORY'S MYSTERIES

SECOND EDITION

RICHARD MORENO

Globe
Pequot

Guilford, Connecticut

Globe
Pequot

An imprint of The Rowman & Littlefield Publishing Group, Inc.
4501 Forbes Blvd., Ste. 200
Lanham, MD 20706
www.rowman.com

Distributed by NATIONAL BOOK NETWORK

British Library Cataloguing in Publication Information available

Library of Congress Cataloging-in-Publication Data available

ISBN 978-1-4930-3982-1 (paperback)
ISBN 978-1-4930-3983-8 (e-book)

CONTENTS

CONTENTS

ACKNOWLEDGMENTS

A very special thanks to Dennis McBride, Guy Louis Rocha, Harry Chalekian, Ronald M. James, Philip I. Earl, David W. Toll, the late, great K. J. Evans (I miss you, my friend), Richard V. Francaviglia, and Martin Griffith for their help, guidance, advice, and inspiration. Also, a shout-out to my wife, Pam, my daughter, Julia, and my son, Hank, who always get me.

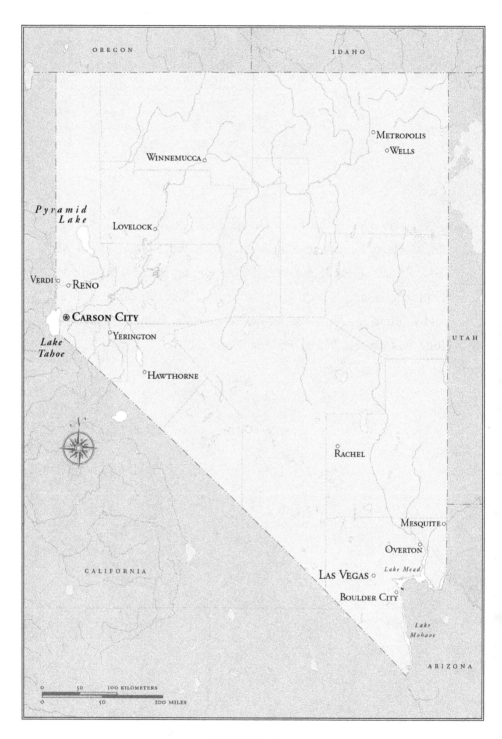

NEVADA

INTRODUCTION

Let us be thankful for the fools.
But for them the rest of us could not succeed.

—Mark Twain

A large part of what makes for a successful mystery or legend is belief. Whether believing that the US government has a secret base in the Nevada desert where it hides alien spacecraft or that gangster Bugsy Siegel singlehandedly conceived of and created Las Vegas, the basis for those realities is believing—fervently—that they are honest-to-God true. And in a place like Nevada, where some people just *know* they can beat the house in every casino, it should not be a surprise that plenty of mysteries and legends not only exist but also are whole-heartedly believed.

A newspaper editor in the classic Western film *The Man Who Shot Liberty Valance* notes that "when the legend becomes fact, print the legend." And that is often the case in Nevada, where some myths are repeated so often that they are believed to be factual. That's why there are people who swear that former Nevada senator Key Pittman really did die before he was re-elected and his body was kept iced in a bathtub (his opponent certainly thought so), as well as why so many folks believe Butch Cassidy and the Sundance

Kid really did rob the First National Bank of Winnemucca in 1900. It's why people drive out to the tiny town of Rachel, Nevada, and set up high-powered telescopes in the hope of seeing a genuine UFO, and the reason treasure hunters with metal detectors still comb the hills near Verdi, Nevada, trying to locate thousands of dollars in lost loot from a long-ago train robbery.

Of course, another reason it's so easy to believe some of the strange tales about Nevada is that it can be such a mysterious place. Let's face it, when you drive deep into Nevada's outback—which is just about any place in the state that isn't named Las Vegas, Lake Tahoe, or Reno—it can be lonely. And empty. And a bit scary. Out there, it's easy to let the imagination run screaming to and from the dark places. All those stories about people falling into old, abandoned mine shafts (which turn out to be true every couple of years), the armies of large, hairy tarantulas crawling across the roads near the town of Gabbs (true during the mating season), and killers like Charles Manson hanging out in Nevada ghost towns (bizarrely enough, also true) certainly give one pause.

The 1940 Works Progress Administration Guide to Nevada described the state as the "great unknown"—and it continues to be true. As one of the most sparsely populated states, it remains a place that has not been fully mapped or explored. Otherwise, someone might have found banker Roy Frisch's body or the half-million dollars' worth of gold coins that are rumored to still be hidden in the hills west of Reno or what really goes on at Area 51.

After all, it just depends on what you're willing to believe.

CHAPTER 1

A Chilling Death

On the evening of November 4, 1940, Nevada Senator Key Pittman was celebrating at the swanky Riverside Hotel in Reno. The veteran lawmaker was running for his sixth term—he won his seat in a 1913 special election after the incumbent died—and was heavily favored to be re-elected. Smug that victory was in the bag, the senator had begun to celebrate early. He invited a handful of his closest political pals to his hotel suite for an all-night poker game and, of course, adult refreshments.

Despite the late hour, the game was lively, with plenty of crude banter and lots of liquor. Through bloodshot eyes, the senator studied his cards. He refilled his glass with another three fingers of a fine, aged whiskey, took a deep swallow, and sat back in an overstuffed leather chair. Confident his cards would trump the others, the senator started to push a small stack of chips to the center of the table.

Then, he stopped. He felt a wave of nausea and a tingling in his fingers. He shook his head, like a dog trying to shake off the rain, but the feeling wouldn't go away. He folded his cards face down on the table and told the others to finish up the hand without him. He said he just needed to lie down for a minute.

As he stood to walk to the bed, there was a sharp pain in his chest. He reached for the table to steady himself but couldn't seem to find it. His knees buckled and he fell to the floor. He was unconscious before his head hit the carpet.

The other players quickly sobered up and were on their feet. One barked for someone to call a doctor. As they waited for help to arrive, they watched the senator lying on the floor, his breathing so shallow, and all had the same thought: What the hell does this mean for the election in a few days?

Eyewitnesses say that evening's festivities had involved lots of drinking—no surprise since Pittman was an alcoholic. According to former Nevada state archivist Guy Louis Rocha, a political confidant wrote to Nevada's other US senator, Patrick McCarran, who disliked the popular Pittman, that the senator had "been drunk practically every day he has been in the state of Nevada, and last Monday night [October 21] he appeared at a Democratic rally in Sparks, at which time he had to hold himself up in order to stand."

As detailed in Ed Reid and Ovid Demaris's 1963 book, *The Green Felt Jungle*, an exposé of organized crime figures in Nevada, what happened next was one of the most bizarre cover-ups in Nevada's political history. In Reid and Demaris's version of events, Pittman suffered a massive heart attack a few days before the election and died. Not wanting Pittman's Republican opponent, Samuel Platt, to win, the state's Democratic Party powerbrokers decided to place the senator's body in a bathtub filled with ice and keep

Nevada US Senator Key Pittman, circa 1913

him there until after the election, when governor Edward Carville, also a Democrat, could name a replacement. Reid and Demaris also incorrectly reported that this occurred at the Mizpah Hotel in Tonopah and not at the Riverside (a "fact" that appeared for many years on the menus of a restaurant in the Mizpah).

Reid and Demaris wrote, "The announcement of his death came a few days after the election and the Republicans attempted to get the story into circulation to circumvent the results of the election."

But is the story true? Rocha believes that there was a cover-up but not the one told in the macabre legend. Rocha, who has studied Pittman's death records and interviewed the doctor who treated the senator, finds that the facts are substantially different from the legend.

Writing in the September-October 1996 issue of *Nevada Magazine*, Rocha said, "According to his death certificate, Pittman officially had died of 'congestive heart failure' at Washoe General Hospital in Reno five days after the election. The certificate and cause of death seemed legitimate, although if a body had been kept on ice somewhere, who would record it?" Rocha showed the death certificate to a mortician, who said that if Pittman had, indeed, been kept on ice for any period of time, the certificate should have made mention of freeze damage to the skin tissue, but there was no such information. Additionally, the embalmer who worked on Pittman's body made no mention of finding the type of tissue damage that would have occurred had it been sitting in ice for any period of time.

The archivist also recognized the name of the attending physician, Dr. A. J. "Bart" Hood, whom he had met several years earlier. He knew that Dr. Hood was retired but still alive and decided to ask him about Pittman's death. According to the doctor, very late on November 4, an aide to the senator called and reported that Pittman had passed out drunk and fell to the floor. Upon arriving at the hotel, Dr. Hood found an obviously inebriated Pittman, who had suffered a massive heart attack.

In the early morning hours, Pittman was surreptitiously moved to the hospital and, at Dr. Hood's insistence, a heart specialist was quickly flown to Reno from San Francisco. The second doctor verified that Pittman had experienced a heart attack and said the senator probably wouldn't survive more than a few days.

Rocha says this is when the real cover-up began. Governor Carville and other Democratic Party leaders were informed of Pittman's grave condition and decided to withhold the information from the public until after the election. By doing this, Governor Carville would be able to appoint another Democrat to replace the dying Pittman, thus assuring the seat would remain safely in Democratic hands. The only inkling that something might be amiss came when the *Nevada State Journal* in Reno reported that Pittman would not be traveling to Tonopah to vote on election day, as he normally did, because he was fatigued from the strain of campaigning and had checked himself in to a Reno hospital to rest for a few days before returning to Washington, D.C. In the paper, Dr. Hood is quoted as saying, "The senator's condition is not critical, but he will be kept in the hospital several days, principally for the rest."

Rocha is blunt in assessing what happened: "Democratic leaders chose to keep the facts secret and issued a cover story that Pittman was temporarily ill, thus allowing Nevadans to go to the polls on November 5 and elect a dying man." Ignorant of Pittman's true condition, Nevada voters overwhelmingly re-elected him by a margin of 31,351 to 20,488 over Platt, a former US attorney who had previously lost twice to the senator (in 1916 and 1928). Not surprisingly, for the rest of his life Platt believed that a dead man had defeated him.

Contrary to the iceman legend, however, Pittman was not yet dead. Mimosa Pittman, the senator's wife, was in Washington, D.C., when she heard about his condition. She arrived in Reno on Election Day and immediately visited him in the hospital. In her diary, she wrote that he was alive and seemed "happy."

But the sixty-eight-year-old Pittman was, of course, far sicker than the public knew. On November 9, he slipped into a coma and died early the next morning. Later that day, President Franklin Roosevelt sent a telegram expressing his condolences at the "sudden and unexpected passing of my old friend Key." Rocha notes that what followed was "the largest state ceremonial funeral in Nevada history." A congressional delegation attended, which included Senator Homer T. Bone of Washington, Senator Alva B. Adams of Colorado, and Senator Carl A. Hatch of New Mexico.

Although it was Pittman's desire to have a memorial on a mountaintop or at the University of Nevada, Reno campus, his widow and friends were unable to raise the funds to carry out his wishes. Pittman biographer Betty Glad notes that a committee was formed at the time of his funeral to raise money, but it floundered. For more than two years, Pittman's body lay in a crypt awaiting an appropriate memorial. In June 1942, Pittman's brother, Vail, wrote to Mimosa Pittman asking her to take some kind of action: "It is my understanding that a body should not be kept there over two years at the outside, and really not that long." Finally, in

1943—nearly three years after Pittman's death—the senator was laid to rest in a double-crypt mausoleum in the Mountain View Cemetery in Reno.

Today, Pittman's remains reside in a simple but elegant aboveground crypt made of stone. On the front, beneath a round, bas-relief of his head are his name, dates of birth and death, and the words, CHAIRMAN OF FOREIGN RELATIONS COMMITTEE OF UNITED STATES SENATE, 1933 UNTIL HIS DEATH. He shares the tomb with his wife, Mimosa, who died in 1952. Strangely, her name can be found nowhere on the building. Adjacent is the more elaborate final resting place of the senator's brother, former Nevada Governor Vail Pittman. Carved into the stone monument are his birth and death dates (1883–1964), his years as governor (1945–1951), and the words, HIS LEADERSHIP SHALL EVER BE REGARDED AS OF THE HIGHEST ORDER. On a pedestal in front of the tomb is a bronze bust of Vail Pittman's head.

Key Pittman's death set in motion a complex series of political maneuvers to determine his successor. Rocha notes that, initially, Governor Carville wanted the appointment for himself. The governor planned to resign and have his lieutenant governor, Maurice Sullivan, appoint him to the seat. However, Carville's wife objected and the idea was soon discarded. Other prominent Democrats let it be known they were interested, including former Governor James J. Scrugham, who was Nevada's congressional representative (in those days, Nevada only had one congressional member); Pittman's younger brother, Vail, who was then publisher of the *Ely Daily Times*; and Al Cahlan, the powerful editor of the *Las Vegas Review-Journal*, who personally lobbied the governor for the appointment and, he later claimed, was told by Carville that he would be selected.

Two weeks after Pittman's death, Governor Carville appointed Berkeley Bunker, speaker of the Nevada State Assembly, to the senate seat. The decision was a surprise to nearly everyone, as Bunker, a Las Vegas service station owner, was relatively young—only thirty-four—and lacked the political heft of most of the other aspirants. However, Bunker was a Mormon bishop and had helped deliver southern Nevada for Carville. At the time, the governor said he made the appointment in the interest of providing geographical balance since McCarran was from Reno. A disappointed Vail, who felt the seat was rightly his, later wrote that Carville selected Bunker in order to appease the growing Mormon vote in southern Nevada.

An interesting postscript is that, in 1945, Governor Carville resigned in order to be appointed to the same, once-again-vacant senate seat. In 1942, Congressman Scrugham defeated Senator Berkeley Bunker in the Democratic primary, and was elected to Pittman's former seat. Three years later, Scrugham died in office, and this time Carville wanted the job. He resigned as governor and was appointed to the seat by his lieutenant governor (who automatically became acting governor). Ironically, the lieutenant governor was Vail Pittman, who had been elected to the position in 1942.

Key Pittman was a colorful and often controversial figure in Nevada's political history. Born in 1872 in Vicksburg, Mississippi, he attended Southwestern Presbyterian University in Tennessee but dropped out for health reasons before completing his degree. He relocated to Seattle, where he was admitted to the Washington bar, and practiced law for several years.

In 1897, he heard the siren call of the Alaska gold rush and headed for the Klondike, where he prospected, practiced law (becoming proficient in mining law), and met his wife, Mimosa. Four years later, the Pittmans headed to San Francisco after Mimosa became sick and was advised to leave the Arctic during the winter. While there, Pittman heard about fabulous mineral discoveries in Tonopah, Nevada. He set out for Central Nevada and, once there, found plenty of work for an ambitious attorney with knowledge of mining laws.

Pittman quickly became one of Tonopah's most prominent lawyers and parlayed his success into a political career. He ran for the US Senate in 1910 but lost to the incumbent, Republican George Nixon. Two years later, Nixon died, and Pittman was narrowly elected by 89 votes to fill out the remainder of the term. Fred L. Israel, who wrote a 1963 biography of Pittman, noted that Pittman "devoted his energies to the needs and interests of his state ... Pittman did not represent the American people but was, instead, the spokesman of his state, safeguarding the interests of 110,000 people from the rest of the 130 million."

Despite his decidedly Nevada-centric focus, Pittman was elected chairman of the Senate Foreign Relations Committee in 1933—not because he had an interest or affinity for foreign affairs but because he was the senior member of the committee. Israel noted that "Pittman was not made for this role. . . . Unlike [previous chairmen] [Charles] Sumner, [Henry Cabot] Lodge, and [William Edgar] Borah, he failed to grasp the fine points of American foreign relations."

Israel recounts that in 1933, President Roosevelt selected Pittman as a delegate at a World Monetary and Economic Conference in London. Pittman was eager to participate because he saw it as an opportunity to promote silver—still the lifeblood of Nevada—as an important part of the international monetary scene. During the six-week conference, attended by 66 nations, the senator was a tireless voice for the re-monetization of silver but showed little interest in any other economic issue.

"Except for silver, Pittman was useless at London," Israel wrote. "Throughout the conference, especially at crucial moments, he would get drunk. While in this condition, his favorite method of amusing himself was to pop the London streetlights with his six-shooter."

As chair of the committee, Pittman proved not to be a rubber stamp for President Roosevelt, particularly—at least initially—when it came to foreign intervention. Additionally, Israel noted, "Pittman's drinking habits sometimes caused the administration considerable embarrassment. . . . Alcohol often caused Pittman to act on rash impulse, failing to grasp the importance of what he was doing. In December 1935, for example, reporters quoted him as saying that Japan's ultimate objective was the conquest of the world."

In its obituary for the senator on November 18, 1940, *Time* magazine wrote that Pittman could be "downright careless with words." The piece noted that he once endorsed sanctions against Italy by saying, "Why shoot a man when you can starve him to death?" *Time*, which erroneously reported that Pittman had fallen ill in the Mizpah Hotel in Tonopah and was transported to a Reno hospital, also noted that the plainspoken Pittman once called Adolf Hitler "a coward."

In *A Short History of Reno*, authors Barbara and Myrick Land report that the origin of the frozen senator legend may have evolved from a casual remark made by one of Pittman's aides, who allegedly told a reporter that the reason the Senator had made so few personal appearances in the last days of the campaign was because his staff was "keeping him on ice."

Certainly, stranger things have happened.

CHAPTER 2

At the Bottom of Lake Tahoe

It was said to be "bigger than the houses of the white man," according to one Native American legend. Its wings were as long as the tallest pine trees at Lake Tahoe. It had a body that resembled an eagle's, but covered with both feathers and scales, and had giant webbed feet. Its head was perhaps its most remarkable feature—it was said to look nearly human.

And it liked the taste of human flesh.

The native Washo Indians, who lived around the lake until the arrival of white settlers in the mid-nineteenth century, called the terrible creature the Ong and said it lived in a nest at the bottom of Lake Tahoe, which sits on the border of Nevada and California. The Ong's nest was said to be the source of the waters that flowed into and out of the lake. In fact, this ebb and flow of the waters was said to explain the great undercurrents found in the deep lake, which scientists have measured to be as deep as 1,645 feet.

The Washo legend, as reported in a 1921 book, *The Lake of the Sky*, by George Wharton James, also noted that the Ong

Richard Moreno

The third deepest lake in North America, Lake Tahoe has been the subject of many myths and legends, including several involving humped sea serpents.

had a voracious appetite. The birdlike monster ate everything it encountered, including Lake Tahoe's fish, birds, animals, and, of course, people.

"No one ever heard or saw anything of such poor mortals as were drowned in these waters, for their bodies were carried to the Ong's nest and no morsel ever escaped him," James wrote. "Sometimes he would fly about the shores in quest of some child or woman or hunter, yet he was a great coward and was never known to attack anyone in camp, or when two or more were together. No arrow could pierce his feathers, nor could the strongest spear do more than glance from the scales on his face and legs, yet his coward's heart made him afraid for his toes had no claws, and his mouth no beak."

In Washo mythology, the tale of the Ong's downfall is intertwined with the story of how Lake Tahoe gained its name. One day the Washo were preparing for their final hunt of the season at the lake, which at that time had no name. During the colder months, the Washo traditionally departed the higher elevations around the lake and moved into the lower valleys of eastern Nevada, where the snow was not so deep during the winter. The chief of the Washo had a sixteen-year-old daughter, Nona, who was the most beautiful girl anyone had ever seen. Because she was of age, it was the Washo custom that before leaving the lake the chief would select the greatest hero of the tribe to be her husband.

For years the tribe's eligible warriors had looked forward to this day and performed increasingly daring acts of heroism in the hope of being selected to wed the chief's daughter. On the morning the tribe was to leave for the lower valleys and the chief was to make his choice known, one particular young brave, who loved the daughter (and she, in return, secretly loved him) knew he was down to his last chance to win her hand in marriage. Because of his young age, he had never been allowed to participate in any of the earlier battles between the Washo and their traditional enemies, the Paiutes, nor had he ever done anything particularly brave or bold that would earn him the distinction of being the tribe's greatest hero.

The brave prayed to the Great Spirit, the name the Washo gave to their creator, for guidance. Just when he was about to give up hope that the spirit would help him, he saw the Ong rise from the lake. As the massive bird flew to the shoreline to look for prey, the brave moved about to catch its attention. The Ong spotted him and swooped down to where he was standing. Other members of the tribe saw this happen and screamed in horror as the Ong grabbed the brave with its webbed feet. Typically, after the bird monster snagged its prey, it would fly high in the sky and then release the victim into the lake and allow the current to carry it to its nest.

But while the Ong was soaring higher, the brave was busy. He unfurled a buckskin rope and bound himself securely to the creature's feet. Once high above the lake, the monster found it could not drop the young man. In frustration, it twisted itself around and tried to bite the brave with its terrible teeth but was unable to reach him. Each time it opened its mouth to snap at him, the brave tossed a handful of poisoned arrows down its throat.

Desperate to rid itself of the brave and feeling the pain of dozens of sharp, toxic arrows piercing its insides, the Ong plunged into the lake. The cord, however, kept its feet tied together so it could not swim. The horrible creature flapped its wings in a great frenzy, causing the lake's waters to foam, but it could not break free. The brave nearly drowned as the animal thrashed about. Finally, with enormous effort, the Ong rose from the lake with the brave in tow and flew to the middle. As the sun disappeared over the mountains and darkness enveloped the lake, the giant bird and the brave seemed to vanish.

The Washo around the lake lit fires and resumed their end-of-summer ceremonies. Once again, the warriors began sharing their stories of bravery and daring accomplishments in the hope of gaining the hand of the chief's beautiful daughter. Nearly all believed that despite the great contest between the monster and the brave, the Ong had claimed yet another victim. But the chief's daughter hoped and prayed for a different outcome. She quietly left the encampment and paddled a small canoe out into the lake. She didn't know why the Ong had not dropped her lover or why the creature had appeared to behave so strangely—none of the tribe's members knew of the rope or the poisoned arrows. Her plan was to go to the middle of the lake to rescue him or, if she could not find him, to join him in death. As she paddled, she softly called out his name, "Tahoe! My darling Tahoe!"

Meanwhile, back at the camp, the stories had ended and the chief called for his daughter to join the council to hear his decision regarding his choice for her husband. When it was discovered that she was gone, there was great consternation in the camp, which lasted throughout the night. At daybreak, however, the tribe was astonished to see the dead body of the Ong floating in the lake above its nest. Beside it was an empty canoe.

As the sun began to rise, the Washo witnessed a miraculous sight: Standing on one of the Ong's mighty wings, with the tip of the other wing serving as a sail, were Tahoe and Nona. The two lovers, clasped in each other's arms, reached the shore where elated members of their tribe embraced them. All proclaimed Tahoe as the hero of heroes—and a worthy husband for the chief's daughter. Furthermore, the lake would carry his name from that day forward. As for the Ong's nest, it still sits there at the bottom of the lake, which is why, it is said, those who drown in the lake never rise to the surface.

But the Ong isn't Lake Tahoe's only monster. A fable of more recent vintage involves a giant lake serpent that has affectionately been called Tahoe Tessie. Although Tessie has mostly been seen as a marketing gimmick to create a Loch Ness Monster knock-off so Tahoe businesses can sell more T-shirts, there *have* been reports of rather unusual sightings in the lake. For instance, the *Reno News and Review* reported an episode in the early 1980s when fisherman Gene St. Denis and his friend were looking into the water near Cave Rock at Lake Tahoe. According to the paper, St. Denis saw "a blotchy gray creature about 10 feet to 15 feet long." He said the strange creature made a sharp turn in the water and created a large V-shaped wake. St. Denis claims he has also hauled in large fish that were severely chewed on while being reeled in. "About halfway to the boat, these fish—they were big fish—got raked," he told the paper. St. Denis has his own theories about what he saw—he claims it's either a giant white sturgeon or river sturgeon, or a massive muskie.

Or something else.

Every year, there are a handful of alleged sightings of some kind of large, serpentine-like creature in the lake. In April 2005, the *Tahoe Daily Tribune* reported that two Sacramento area visitors, Beth Douglas and Ron Talmadge, caught sight of a dark, undulating shape in the waters off Tahoe Park Beach. Douglas told the paper that she had seen something large and long that seemed to have three to five humps along its back. Talmadge was quoted as saying, "Damn, that's Tessie . . . I thought, 'Whoa, this sucker's real.'"

Additionally, several websites claim that the famed ocean-ographer, Jacques Cousteau, came to Lake Tahoe in the 1970s and explored the bottom of the lake with a special, motorized submersible. What he found was said to be so horrible that afterward he vowed never to show the film footage to anyone or to speak of it. In 2004, the *San Francisco Chronicle* repeated the story about Cousteau's visit to Tahoe in the mid-'70s, adding that when asked about it, the renowned explorer allegedly said, "The world isn't ready for what was down there."

Some say that while Cousteau didn't encounter Tessie, he found perfectly preserved bodies at the lake's bottom, including drowned Chinese woodcutters as well as the fully intact bodies of the victims of gangland killings. While the Cousteau tale is obviously tantalizing, former Nevada state archivist Guy Louis Rocha, who enjoys poking holes in urban myths, has written that the story couldn't be true because there are no records showing that Cousteau—who was quite famous and unlikely to be able to slip in and out of any place without being noticed—ever visited Lake Tahoe or conducted any sort of exploration of the lake.

Additionally, Rocha cites Dr. Graham Kent of the Scripps Institute of Oceanography in San Diego, who notes that no matter how cold and dark it was at the bottom of the lake, there is no way a dead body could remain intact. Dr. Graham says the lake's fish and bottom-dwelling crawdads as well as indigenous bacteria would dine on the bodies.

There are, of course, skeptics when it comes to the existence of Tessie. Professor Charles Goldman of the University of California at Davis, who has studied the lake for more than four decades, scoffs at those who insist that Lake Tahoe is home to any type of lake monster. Goldman told the Associated Press that after years of looking, he has yet to find any concrete evidence that any creature like Tessie lives in the lake. He admitted the most difficult part of trying to verify the existence of a lake monster "is that you can prove something is there, but you can't prove something is not there."

During a 2004 lecture on unidentified swimming objects, Goldman noted, "We think that a lot of the Tessie reports are actually colliding boat wakes [that] produce a series of waves." He said those waves could appear to be humps, particularly to someone with a vivid imagination. "Tessie's like Santa Claus. It's a fun story," he said during his talk.

Dead bodies and monsters aren't the only stories told about Lake Tahoe. In the nineteenth century, it was often believed that the lake was so deep that it either had no bottom or had a tunnel at its bottom that led to some other body of water. One of the best hoaxes about what lies at the bottom of Lake Tahoe came from newspaper editor Sam Davis's story, "The Mystery of the Savage Sump." Published in 1901, the tale describes a badly decomposed body that mysteriously appears in a sump [a drainage hole] inside the Savage Mine in Virginia City. According to Davis, the man was an unsuccessful mining stock speculator from San Francisco named William Meeker. One day while vacationing at Lake Tahoe, Meeker noticed how the water near Carnelian Bay on the lake seemed to swirl, as if there was a subterranean outlet deep beneath the surface.

He carved his initials on a wooden stick to which he attached a weight and some line. He dropped it into the lake and, according to Davis, "It went down in about a hundred feet of water and then something began bearing it down. There was a succession of tugs and the line began spinning over the edge of the boat with rapidly increasing speed. The line caught on the boat and snapped with the strain. This made it clear to him that the water was surging through an outlet in the lake bottom."

After returning to San Francisco, Meeker shared his findings with an associate, Colonel Clair, whom Davis described as "one of the heaviest and most unscrupulous operators in the market." The two studied maps and surveys and determined that the hole eventually emptied into Virginia City's underground silver mines, which often filled with hot, underground water that had to be pumped out at great expense.

The two developed a scheme to buy up stock in one of the mines that their research indicated was an exit for water flowing into the hole in the lake—the Savage Mine. After snatching up thousands of inexpensive shares of Savage Mine stock—and telling everyone that the mine would never be profitable as long as it was filled with water—they plugged the hole, which caused the water levels to drop, thereby making the mine's lower levels more accessible. Word soon spread about the fabulous new deposits exposed by the drop in the water level, and suddenly every broker wanted to buy shares in the Savage. Throughout the frenzy, Colonel Clair quietly sold his shares in small lots, earning about a million dollars. At the peak of the stock's value, Colonel Clair began buying short, meaning he would only make money if the stock value were to drop. The two then unplugged the hole, which caused the mine to again fill with water—and the stock crashed. In this way, Colonel Clair made another million.

For a time, they continued this practice of buying and selling the mine's stock while controlling the ebb and flow of the water, and they became extremely wealthy. But Colonel Clair wanted it all for himself. One night, as Meeker was raising the plug, the Colonel slammed an iron bar into his partner's head, killing him instantly. He tied a weight to Meeker's body and dumped it into the lake, where it was sucked into the hole and eventually made its way to the sump in the Savage Mine.

Davis said the discovery of Meeker's water-logged and decomposed body in the mine sump revealed the existence of the drainage tunnel between the mine and the lake and was all the evidence needed to shut down Colonel Clair's scheme. While Davis's story was clearly fiction, it didn't stop the plethora of legends about the hole in the bottom of the lake—and in some cases was cited as proof the hole existed. Stories still circulate about the existence of some type of underground passage linking the lake to another body of water, Pyramid Lake, which is 45 miles north of Reno. Some say that's why the bodies of drowning victims are never found in Lake Tahoe and allegedly later show up in Pyramid Lake—although that more likely has more to do with the fact the two lakes are connected by the Truckee River, which flows out of Lake Tahoe and into Pyramid Lake.

In the end, whether monsters, well-preserved dead bodies, or bottomless holes, perhaps the things that Lake Tahoe truly has in abundance are stories and tall tales.

Ever hear about the time Bigfoot was sighted at Lake Tahoe?

CHAPTER 3

Lovelock's Redheaded Giants

John T. Reid was a believer. As a boy growing up in Lovelock, he had befriended many of the local Paiutes, including Natchez, son of Chief Winnemucca, the venerable leader of the northern Nevada Paiutes. He would often hear their wondrous stories, which included tales of a long and bloody war between the Paiutes and a race of giant man-eating, red-haired Indians called the Si-te-cah, who had come from the south.

And he believed.

He was shown a cave south of Lovelock, which, he was told, was the scene of a siege during which the Paiutes finally killed the last of the Si-te-cah, which in the Paiute language translates as "redheaded tule eaters." In his private papers, he later described his first visit to the cave, now known as Lovelock Cave. In one manuscript, he said that in 1886, when he was about fifteen years old, he was rounding up wild horses with several Paiute friends, including Natchez, when it began to rain. To escape the downpour, the group made camp on a flat below the cave. When he suggested they enter

Mining engineer and geologist John T. Reid, who, in the 1920s, claimed to have found the bones of prehistoric giant red-haired Indians in a Northern Nevada cave.

the cave to get out of the rain, he was told that Paiutes never go into the cave because it contained evil spirits.

Natchez proceeded to tell the young Reid that many years ago a tribe of men, whom he described as "very tall" and having red hair, entered the Paiutes' territory. The intruders proved to be hostile, attacking the Paiutes without cause and, it was said, eating the bodies of anyone they captured or killed. War ensued and eventually the surviving redheaded giants holed up in the cave. To draw them out, the Paiutes stacked dried sagebrush at the mouth of the cave and lit a fire. Whenever the interlopers tried to escape the smoke-filled cave, the Paiutes shot them with their bows and arrows.

"After a siege lasting several days, Natches [*sic*] relates that all of the intruders were dead," Reid wrote.

A version of Natchez's story about the red-haired giants also appeared in Sarah Winnemucca's classic book, *Life Among the Paiutes: Their Wrongs and Claims*, published in 1883. Winnemucca, the first Native American woman to author a book, told of a "small tribe of barbarians who lived along the Humboldt River." She said members of the group would "waylay" her people and eat them. Winnemucca wrote that finally there was a war between the two tribes, which lasted some three years.

According to Winnemucca, during the war the Paiutes killed all but a small group of the aggressors, who fled inside the Lovelock Cave. Her people piled up wood at the cave's entrance and asked those inside to surrender. Not receiving any response, they set the wood on fire and killed everyone inside.

"My people say that the tribe we exterminated had reddish hair," she wrote. "I have some of their hair, which has been handed down from father to son. I have a dress which has been in our family a great many years, trimmed with this reddish hair . . . it is called the mourning dress, and no one has such a dress but my family."

The story stayed with Reid, who grew up to become a successful mining engineer and geologist. He also dabbled in inventing things. In 1919, he received US patents for two devices—one for a giant bladder that inflated to keep a damaged boat afloat and the other for a seagoing vessel that carried its cargo below the water level. However, Reid's frequent excursions into the northern Nevada backcountry looking for minerals were the catalyst for what became his real passions: fossil hunting and archaeology. As he hiked through the dry, sagebrush-covered mountains around Lovelock, he often looked for arrowheads, pottery shards, and any other keys that might unlock the secrets of the past.

In the early 1920s, he ignited a small firestorm of controversy when he reported being given a piece of rock from the Triassic period (about 250 to 200 million years ago) near Fisher Canyon, outside of Lovelock, that appeared to contain the imprint of a human shoe print. A March 19, 1922, article in the *New York Sunday American*, entitled "Mystery of the Petrified Shoe Sole," reported, somewhat breathlessly, that "while prospecting for fossils in Nevada, John T. Reid, a distinguished mining engineer and geologist, stopped suddenly and looked down in utter bewilderment and amazement at a rock near his feet. For there, a part of the rock itself, was what seemed to be a human footprint! Closer inspection showed that it was not a mark of a naked foot, but was, apparently, a shoe sole which had been turned into stone."

He followed that up with another find—a petrified horse's hoof—that the *New York Times* said refuted the relatively new theories of evolutionists (the famous "Scopes Monkey Trial" didn't happen until 1925). In its March 9, 1924, issue, the *Times* said Reid had acquired the foot from a train engineer, who found it in a pile of coal. According to the newspaper, Reid "recognized it as the petrified remains of a horse's right forefoot, and as he said, that broke all the rules since horses, and a modern horse at that, shouldn't have been around at the time of coal formation, according to evolutionists."

Eventually, both fossils were revealed to be nothing more than interestingly shaped rocks—accidents of nature—and not proof of either the existence of leather-shoe-wearing men walking around 200 million years ago or dinosaur-era contemporary-size horses. Despite those findings, it is interesting to note that Reid's photos and reports of the petrified shoe and stone horse hoof still continue to be cited as proof that the theory of evolution is a crock by various creationism websites.

Reid, however, is remembered today more for his involvement in the excavations of Lovelock Cave and the bones subsequently found buried there. In the late 1890s, he began agitating for various academic institutions to conduct a formal exploration of the cave, which he had visited as a boy. Remembering all the Indian stories that he had been told about the cave, he began to wonder if there was any truth to them.

"By this time, he had become convinced that the Indians' recurring references to the redheaded people bore looking into and he began documenting their statements, often in planned interviews complete with witnesses," wrote Dorothy P. Dansie in the Fall 1975 issue of *Nevada Historic Society Quarterly*. Dansie added that many of the tales collected by Reid mentioned that the redheaded intruders were usually extraordinarily tall—as high as 9 feet in height in some versions.

Circa 1911, miners began to extract the rich guano (bat droppings) deposits found in Lovelock Cave. During the course of removing the guano, which was used as fertilizer, the miners found Native American artifacts. According to later reports, the miners tried to get various universities and the Smithsonian Institution to come collect the items, but all declined, saying they did not have funding for such work. Finally, in the fall of 1911, the Nevada State Historical Society in conjunction with the University of California sent an investigator, L. L. Loud, to the site. His later report noted that by the time he arrived, "many objects had been destroyed by the weather and others had been taken away. I recall many boas or ropes of fine feathers. As these lay strewn about in the open end of the cave in the way of the workmen, they were irreparably damaged."

Loud, however, also reported that the cave contained a number of human skeletons. He wrote, "In the north-central part of the cave, about 4 feet deep, was a striking-looking body of a man, 6 feet 6 inches tall. His body was mummified and his hair distinctly red." He said there were also four or five other, smaller mummies, all with red hair. He hypothesized that the more diminutive bodies were women because of their size and the fact they were wearing long, buckskin gowns.

Although Reid had no direct involvement in Loud's work or a later excavation of the cave in 1924 by M. R. Harrington, which was sponsored by the Museum of the American Indian (Heye Foundation) of New York City, he continued his own inquiries. He interviewed dozens of old-timers, including Native American elders, and meticulously recorded what each had to say.

"Tantalizing bits and pieces of information, skeletal fragments of an unusual nature, cunningly crafted artifacts which seemed alien in the land of hunters and gatherers, all served to keep Reid on tetherhooks," Dansie wrote, adding, "to keep him anticipating the discovery which would astound the world and draw to Nevada scientists from far and wide for research."

And it soon came. First, he became convinced that several skulls he had uncovered in the vicinity of the cave were those of prehistoric Neanderthals. After various experts, to whom he had sent the skulls, had dismissed that contention, he set his sights on discovering one of the legendary redheaded giants. In February 1931, he finally stumbled on his holy grail. A local resident told him of a huge skeleton that had become unearthed by the wind and rain in a dry lake bed near Lovelock Cave. Reid went to the site and found the remains. Believing they were, indeed, proof of one of his giants, he measured the bones in situ (situated in their original position) before carefully excavating the site. He later wrote that they were "7 feet, 7 or 6 inches in height. The difference of 1 inch . . . is due to the matter of being unable to determine if the toes, lying upward, had been bent or were erect."

The local newspaper, *the Lovelock Review-Miner*, reported in its June 19, 1931, issue that a man named Lloyd De La Montoya of California had uncovered the remains of what appeared to be a "giant" on the playa southwest of Lovelock. Reid joined two other men, John Foster and Thomas Chapel, and drove to the site mentioned by Montoya. Along the way, their vehicle hit a deep hole. Chapel was thrown from the car and died. Reid and Foster, however, were not seriously injured. Despite the tragedy, Reid continued his research and on a subsequent visit recovered the skeleton. According to reports, the bones were those of a man who had been 9½ to 10 feet tall.

In 1939, Reid had one more opportunity to study the bones of a giant. A local farmer had uncovered another buried skeleton while plowing some land west of Lovelock. Reid was shown the site and began measuring the bones. When he was finished, he told the *Lovelock Review-Miner* that by his calculations the individual had been 7 feet 7 inches in height. In other words: yet another giant.

And with that, there were no more reports about Reid or any further amazing discoveries. On August 20, 1943, at the age of seventy-two, he died in his home after being ill for several weeks. In 1948, his brother sold to the Nevada Historical Society several crates of Reid's private papers and research as well as boxes of fossils, rocks, skulls, and bones, including the skeleton of at least one of Reid's mythical giants.

And that's where the story ended for nearly four decades. According to a Winter 1984 article in the *Nevada Historic Society Quarterly* by Sheilagh Brooks, Carolyn Stark, and Richard H. Brooks, "Over the years the skeletal portion of the Reid Collection was apparently misplaced." Without the bones, the giant redheaded Indians discovered by John Reid became the stuff of urban—or perhaps, in this case, rural—legend.

It was not until 1977, during a makeover of the Nevada Historical Society's main gallery that staff discovered several improperly marked boxes, including those containing the lost Reid skeletons. Now identified, they were sent for analysis to the physical anthropology lab at the University of Nevada, Las Vegas. In 1980, the results were revealed at the Great Basin Anthropological Conference in Salt Lake City.

It turned out Reid was wrong. In measuring the leg bones to gauge the original height of the individuals, he had compared them to his own thigh. The Brooks, Stark, and Brooks article said he had made a common error. "People commonly estimate their thigh lengths from the region of the crotch to the knee ... the head of the thigh bone or femur inserts in the appropriate pelvic socket some 4 to 6 inches above the crotch. If the femoral head is placed at the crotch (like Reid had done), the end of the bone will extend some 4 to 6 inches or more below the knee, and the assumption will then be that this was an extraordinarily tall individual, possible a giant."

The analysis showed that the actual size of the individuals in Reid's collection were average in height, with the males measuring (from tallest to shortest) about 5 feet 11 inches tall to 5 feet 5 inches tall. Certainly not the bones of giants.

Additionally, scientists had an explanation for the red hair on the skulls. Reid's collection included several of the mummified skeletons that appeared to have red or reddish-brown hair. According to Brooks, Stark, and Brooks, there were several possible explanations for the unusual coloring, including the fact that many Great Basin Indians "painted themselves while alive, and also painted their dead, with red ochre ... red ochre also will color hair, changing black hair into a reddish or rusty-brown shade." Additionally, after a body is buried, during the period when it is drying out or starting to disintegrate, the tissues release fluids containing ammonia, which can dye black hair a reddish or orange-colored tint.

"This reddish or rusty-brown coloring for the hair of mummies is not unusual in regions where the natural aridity of the climate has preserved the bodies and the hair," they wrote, adding, "Although the belief in Redheaded Giants will no doubt continue, the John T. Reid Collection does not provide physical evidence to support this tale, nor do the burials recovered from the Lovelock Cave."

So, as much as John Reid wanted to believe in his boyhood legends about man-eating, redheaded giants in northern Nevada, it turned out they just weren't true. The jury, however, is still out on whether his inflatable boat saver or underwater transport ship were such bad ideas.

CHAPTER 4

Pyramid Lake's Water Babies and Other Spirits

Years ago, when I was a reporter at a Reno newspaper, one of my colleagues asked a Pyramid Lake Paiute woman, who worked in the circulation department, if she had ever considered living on the shores of Pyramid Lake. After all, he said, it was a beautiful lake and since the land surrounding it was Paiute Reservation land, did she ever think about building a house on the lake to take advantage of the great views?

The woman, in fact, had just built a new home in Nixon, a small community located about 6 miles south of the lake. She laughed and asked my friend if he was crazy. She said that she had several small children and there was no way she would live close to that lake.

"Why?" he asked.

"Because of the water babies," she explained. "They would come take away my children."

That, in a nutshell, is the power of legends. The native Paiutes, who lived for centuries at Pyramid Lake, have many stories that

Sketch of Pyramid Lake from John C. Frémont's report of his 1844 expedition through Nevada

COURTESY OF THE NEVADA HISTORICAL SOCIETY

relate to the desert body of water, which serves as the end point for the Truckee River that flows out of Lake Tahoe, but none quite as frightening—or as powerful—as those involving water babies.

According to the most common version of the myth, the water babies are evil spirits that live in Pyramid Lake, a 27-mile-long and 4- to 11-mile-wide body of water located about 33 miles northeast of Reno. Nevada historian Robert McCracken has written that water babies are a "water spirit of evil disposition." He said they typically dwell in streams and lakes but venture forth at night to steal children that are left unguarded by their parents. It is said that in the evening the cries of these spirits can be heard coming from Pyramid Lake, tempting young children to come out to play.

In his book *Believing in Place: A Spiritual Geography of the Great Basin*, Richard V. Francaviglia wrote, "Water babies are potent spirits who lure the unwary to death and destruction. As recounted by a Shoshone woman: 'When you hear the crying [of the water babies], it means someone is going to die.'" Francaviglia also related another story about how water babies would sometimes trick nursing mothers by taking the place of their babies. "When the baby cried, the woman would pick it up and nurse it," he wrote. "But that was when the water baby would reveal its truly terrible character." He said that the creature would first swallow the woman's breast, and then the entire woman.

Water babies are also said to be the reason that swimming in the lake can be dangerous. According to the legends, the babies grab at the legs and feet of swimmers and pull them underwater—until they drown. Of course, as with many legends, there may be a valid reason behind the story. The lake can be a treacherous place to swim because it has a severe undertow, which can drag a swimmer, particularly a young one, under the waves or far out into the lake to drown. The lake bed is also tricky—shallow and perfect for wading in some spots but suddenly deep and dangerous in others (it is 356 feet at its deepest point). It's not a stretch to believe that the legends about water babies might have evolved to scare young children into giving the lake a wide berth or to at least treat it with caution.

In any event, the Paiutes have a healthy respect for the lake. "I used to tell my children, when you go to the lake, bless the water first. Wash your face with the water, then you can swim in the lake," noted one tribe member, Mamie John, in the Inter-Tribal Council of Nevada's official history of the Northern Paiutes.

Because it's a desert lake, Pyramid Lake's surface water temperature is much warmer than the temperature of water closer to the bottom, reportedly as cold as 38 degrees in the deeper parts.

As a result, the lake, just like Lake Tahoe, is reluctant to give up its dead. Over the decades, there have been dozens of stories about people drowning in the lake whose bodies are never recovered because they sink to the bottom and are held there by the colder water. As recently as 2007, a man in a boat fell overboard without a life jacket and drowned in Pyramid Lake. After several days of searching, rescue teams abandoned their efforts because it had become obvious that the body would never be found.

At least one unique creature lives in the lake—the prehistoric cui-ui fish. The cui-ui (pronounced qwe-we) is a gray-brown, bony suckerfish that lives only in Pyramid Lake. An endangered species, the cui-ui eats algae and other small organisms in the lake and can grow to about 2 feet in length. The species is believed to have been around for more than 2 million years. Reflecting the fish's importance, the Pyramid Lake Paiutes call themselves the "Cuiyui Ticutta," or cui-ui eaters.

Since the 1970s, the Paiute tribe, working with the support of the federal government, has spent millions of dollars trying to re-establish the cui-ui in the lake. Those efforts have been somewhat thwarted by the lake's increasing salinity levels—a dam constructed in the early twentieth century has diverted most of the Truckee River's traditional flow into the lake to agricultural lands in other parts of the state—although the general fish population is holding steady at the present time.

Additionally, another species of endemic fish, the Lahontan cutthroat trout, was completely wiped out in the 1940s by both overfishing and the loss of fresh water flowing into the lake (flows were so low that the fish could not spawn in the river). The fish were once so plentiful that in the early twentieth century, the lake supported several commercial fishing operations. In 1925, a Paiute fisherman caught a Lahontan cutthroat, which weighed a world-record 41 pounds. In recent decades, the species, which managed to survive at Walker Lake, has been reintroduced via hatchlings raised in a fishery operated by the Paiute tribe. The fish, however, remain on the federal list of threatened species.

Part of what makes all the strange stories about Pyramid Lake believable is its appearance. Largely devoid of any type of vegetation, it just looks different from most other bodies of water—despite being the second largest natural lake in the West with a surface area of about 183 square miles. The lake has a salinity level that is about one-sixth seawater (the high salt content in the soil prevents most plants from growing).

Since the lake has long been part of Paiute culture and tradition, it should be no surprise that there are plenty of other legends involving it. For example, the distinctive pyramid-shaped rock that protrudes from the lake and gives it its name is said to be the spearhead of the Great Father, who allegedly thrust it upward to ward off a long drought. Explorer John C. Frémont named the lake during his 1844 expedition through the region. He saw the 500-foot-high triangular rock jutting from the lake's waters and wrote that it reminded him of the Great Pyramid of Giza. Frémont also wrote about enjoying the lake's cutthroat trout, which he said were large, plentiful, and amazingly easy to catch.

The pyramid rock, along with dozens of other unusual stone formations around the lake, are made of tufa, a rock formed thousands of years ago when calcium-rich springs bubbled up through the lake's salty, carbonated water. The chemical bonding of the two substances results in the creation of the limestone-like material called tufa. Only when the water receded and the tufa was exposed to air did these formations cease to grow. In addition to the pyramid, which sits off the southeast end of the lake, there are many other tufa sculptures, all of which contribute to the lake's otherworldly ambience.

For example, on the southeastern edge of the lake are several large, mushroom-shaped tufa forms. Visitors can climb into the hollow centers of these strange, mysterious domes and get a nice view of the pyramid. According to a US Geological Survey report, these 'shroom stones are composed of "layers of broccoli-like branching tufa and dense tufa noodles."

Additionally, just south of the mushroom patch is Great Stone Mother and Basket, a remarkable tufa formation that resembles a giant, hooded Indian woman seated next to an open basket. While there are several variations of the legend of Stone Mother, the most common one is that once upon a time the first woman was married to the first man, who was the father of all Indians. They had many children but their firstborn was a boy who was a troublemaker, always fighting with his siblings. The father grew tired of the bickering, so he called all of the children together and told them that if they did not stop fighting he would be forced to separate them.

Even before he finished speaking, the oldest boy and the other children started to argue. The father became angry and told them that they could no longer live together. He said he was going to return to his home in the sky and only when each of them died would they be allowed to join him there by following the trail of stars (the Milky Way). He called out to the oldest boy, paired him with one of the sisters, and sent them west. They became the Pitt River Indians. He saw that the other children had not started the trouble, so he told them they could stay at home, but they would have to take care of their mother. They became the Paiute people. Then, the father went into the mountains and returned to his home in the sky.

Although treated well by her children, the woman greatly missed her banished son and daughter. One day, she sat with her back to a mountain and gazed west. She was heartbroken as she thought of her missing children and began to cry. Each day, she sat next to her basket and cried. Eventually, her tears fell so fast and furiously that a lake began to form around her. This puddle grew into Pyramid Lake. According to the legend, she sat and cried for so long that she and her basket turned to stone. Today, she still sits—forever preserved in tufa—on the eastern shore of the lake, awaiting the return of her children.

In addition to the big pyramid, the tufa domes, and Stone Mother, the shores of Pyramid Lake contain other unusual formations and, in a few places, small caves. While there aren't any legends or myths associated with them, they add to the lake's mystique. In most cases, names reflect physical characteristics, such as Indian Head Rock, which looks like—you guessed it—the profile of an Indian's head. Similarly, the tufa formations at Popcorn Rocks are shaped like big kernels of popped corn (as well as giant tubes) while the Needles Rocks, also known as the Pinnacles, are tall and somewhat pointy.

Another of Pyramid Lake's more unique features is Anaho Island, located near the lake's east shore. The 247-acre island, also made of tufa, is a national wildlife refuge that serves as a sanctuary for colonial nesting birds, primarily American white pelicans. The island is off-limits to people but home to dozens of birds including cormorants, California gulls, great blue herons, and snowy egrets, in addition to the pelicans.

Geologically speaking, Pyramid Lake is a remnant of an ancient inland sea that scientists have named prehistoric Lake Lahontan. Until about 11,000 years ago, this lake covered much of Northern and Central Nevada.

Presumably there were a lot more water babies back then.

CHAPTER 5

The Garden of Eden in Nevada

He later named it the romantic-sounding Hill of a Thousand Tombs and claimed it was the mythical Garden of Eden, where Adam and Eve once frolicked. Geologist and engineer Captain Alan Le Baron knew he had stumbled on something special when, in 1923, he visited the hill overlooking the East Walker River in a remote valley about 30 miles south of Yerington, Nevada. He looked at the terrain, which certainly resembled the dry, desert climates mentioned in the Bible, and saw possibilities. All around him were piles of large boulders and stones carved with thousands of symbols, strange writings, and images of long-extinct animals. On the ground were bones that—it appeared to Le Baron—were from prehistoric camels, lions, and elephants, as well as "petrified remains" of once-lush forests. To the amateur archaeologist, the symbol-covered boulders resembled an ancient burial site.

The place was unlike anything he had seen before in North America. Sure, he had lived in Egypt and spent time in Mesopotamia—his father was a member of the British Funding

Commission in Egypt, which financed archaeological digs in that country—but this was different. Le Baron had learned of the site from a Nevada miner named Frank Bovard. After realizing that the prospector might have stumbled onto something extraordinary, Le Baron set out to the location as soon as possible. Once there, he found thousands of the unusual writings and drawings, which he was convinced were identical to Egyptian and Babylonian characters.

He made drawings and took photographs of the site, which he shared with "Arabian scholars in Egypt," who, he later wrote, agreed with his findings. "The writings have been checked by every method at my command and I am prepared to say positively that this is not the work of Indians," he explained. After returning from his remarkable find, he approached the William Randolph Hearst–owned *San Francisco Examiner* to underwrite a more thorough expedition to the site, which he also called Cascadia.

In spring 1924, Le Baron returned to the site with a group that included Edward Clark, the *Examiner*'s Sunday editor, as well as Dr. H. R. Fairclough, professor of classical literature at Stanford University. He proudly showed the setting, the writings, the rocks, and the bones to the others, who were appropriately impressed.

"We have found what appears to be the evidence of the oldest civilization in the world—the oldest writing, the oldest art, the oldest sacrifice, the oldest worship, and the oldest burial," Clark wrote in the August 17, 1924, edition of the *Examiner*, which announced Le Baron's findings to the world under the banner headline, "Was the Garden of Eden Located in Nevada?" Clark added that the *Examiner*'s expedition was definitely on the trail of a primitive culture that would prove that the "white race had its origin somewhere in western America."

For his part, Dr. Fairclough's later report noted that the discovery was of great importance and he hoped that human remains would eventually be found at the site. Fairclough wrote, "I should not be at all surprised if ultimately it will be found that the earliest human life in America was in some such region as that of Nevada; nor should I be surprised if some evidence would be found carrying the antiquity of man on this continent back to quite as early a period as that claimed in Europe or Asia."

The *Examiner's* excited coverage of the archaeological expedition covered the entire front page of that August 17 issue, as well as several full pages inside. Additionally, a newspaper editorial patted itself on the back for its role in funding the expedition and applauded the "amazing" findings. Subsequent stories on August 18 and August 19 provided large black-and-white photographs of the rock writings and had headlines that stated "Nevada Carvings Are Like Egyptian Hieroglyphs" and "The 'Hill of a Thousand Tombs,' Ancient Burial Site." The latter included an extensive chart showing how the Nevada carvings were identical to the writings of the ancients. Clark's adjacent article cited Grafton Elliott Smith, professor of anatomy at the University College of London and an expert on Egyptian mummies, who "caught at a glance the Babylonian and Egyptian resemblances." According to Clark, who was not averse to hyperbole, Smith studied pictures of the drawings and immediately proclaimed, "No such monument has ever before been reported in this continent . . . nothing like it has ever been found; it is isolated and in a region where none but Indians were known to have lived."

An August 19 article entitled "Hill of a Thousand Tombs" was particularly breathy, with an opening paragraph that simply exclaimed, "Paradise regained!" The article, also by Clark, explained that the presence of so many sun symbols on the rocks, according to Le Baron, was because the site was clearly a "place of worship" and the fact there were frequent depictions of the heads and forms of mountain sheep was proof that it was an altar used for sacrificing animals to some prehistoric gods.

Le Baron said the rock carvings there were sufficiently similar to Egyptian writing that he could make a partial translation. "It said in effect that three hundred young people had returned to the site and it was the burial place of the fathers," Clark reported.

The story also noted that Le Baron was convinced the boulders on the hill covered thousands of tombs, and he had workers dig a shaft on flat, sandy ground between the base of the hill and the East Walker River. Unfortunately, at about 30 feet, water began pouring into the shaft and the project was abandoned. At the top of the hill, Le Baron, Clark, and the others in the group found a large, pear-shaped rock that was balanced point down on a smaller stone. They believed this was proof of "careful masonry construction, without hewn stone or cement," and believed that it was definitely a tomb, carefully sealed to preserve the contents inside. Clark wrote that it appeared "you could roll that stone away like the one that was rolled from the tomb of Christ."

The group deduced that every boulder on the hill covered a tomb—hence the name they gave the place—and decided to dig beneath one of the smaller rocks. "We removed the stones and started digging beneath them with a prospector's pick and our bare hands. Beneath the layers of brown stones we found sand and suddenly the blue-grayness changed to a yellowish white," Clark wrote.

He added that the yellow dust was clearly the "dust of a human dead longer than any scientist dare guess." As he let the yellow dust fall between his fingers and blow from the palm of his hand, he said the experience was "one of indescribable awe." He said that Le Baron, however, wanted more: The explorer wanted bones that could be studied by an anthropologist and not merely dust. He reported a brief debate between members of the group: "'No more for me today,' said I [Clark], still under the spell of the discovery. 'Dust to dust' had a real meaning now. Why disturb any more of the sleepers? They might not like it. 'But it's only their dust—their souls aren't here,' he [Le Baron] responded, arguing against my whim. 'And,' injected Campbell dryly, 'if they've been rocked in for a million years it's time they were let free.' But I carried my point. There was no more digging that day."

A sidebar to the main story quoted Dr. Frank T. Green, a professor of chemistry at the College of Chemistry in San Francisco and a toxicologist for the San Francisco coroner's office, saying that he had analyzed the yellowish dust found at the Hill of a Thousand Tombs and determined "beyond any question of doubt" that it contained calcium phosphate, which is found in bones.

And it wasn't just scientists who embraced Le Baron's discoveries. In 1925, *Theosophy* magazine, published by the Theosophical Society, a religious/philosophy group that incorporates aspects of Eastern and Western religions as well as mystical beliefs, such as reincarnation and the existence of Atlantis, said that Le Baron's discoveries in Cascadia "have suddenly cut the Gordian knot by providing a new center of racial origin." The article said the pictographs found by Le Baron were identical in form to Egyptian, Chaldean, Babylonian, Chinese, and Arabian symbols, and they were proof of the "Wisdom-Religion [the ancient root religion of Theosophy] from which all minor faiths branched and which in its purity survives today as Theosophy."

The article said the writing was clearly ancient because the pictures depicted dinosaurs and other extinct forms of life. Additionally, the presence of desert varnish—the shiny brownish coating found on the rocks that makes the carved images and symbols appear more pronounced—was evidence of volcanic action, which again could only have occurred many tens of thousands of years ago. It suggested that this new evidence about the location of the origin of man would be the "death warrant" for those theories that place the Garden of Eden in Asia or the Middle East, because it was clearly in America.

As naive and incredible as Le Baron's theories seem today, they appeared at a time when the American public was ready to believe. Historical geographer Richard V. Francaviglia, who wrote about Le Baron's discovery in *Believing in Place: A Spiritual Geography of the Great Basin*, noted that the idea of a North American Garden of Eden had deep roots in the American psyche. He wrote that in the 1830s, Joseph Smith, founder of the Mormon Church, had a revelation that the Garden of Eden's location was in Independence, Missouri. According to Francaviglia, "In the Great Basin, faith and landscape conspire to resurrect old myths and create new ones."

The *Examiner's* main editorial on August 19, 1924, predicted, "We of the West are privileged to be present at the birth of this astounding discovery. We are enabled to watch, from the beginning, the debate that seems destined to turn the whole world of science topsy-turvy and to make the year 1924 lastingly memorable for its new knowledge of mankind."

Unfortunately for Le Baron and the *Examiner*, this "lastingly memorable" discovery proved illusory. For a time, Le Baron was a bit of a celebrity; old-timers in Yerington still recall him as a charming gentleman who was always attentive to ladies. He even managed to woo and marry a local schoolteacher, Georganne Kaufman , although the union didn't last. Harry A. Chalekian, who wrote about Le Baron and the Garden of Eden in the July-August 1993 issue of *Nevada Magazine*, noted that eventually Le Baron disappeared from the public eye. "He was last seen working with a road crew on a highway project between Fernley and Yerington," Chalekian said.

Over the years, other experts, curious about the hype, have visited the site, studied the rock writing, the tombs, and the bones and determined that the Babylonian and Egyptian "hieroglyphics" were actually prehistoric Native American petroglyphs—carved by those same Indians that Le Baron dismissed—while the bones (and bone dust) were nothing more than the remains of ancient indigenous species such as sheep, deer, and rabbits. The rock writing wasn't even as ancient as Le Baron believed. Scientists now say it dates back about 2,000 to 3,000 years, and some is more recent, having been made 800 to 1,000 years ago. Ironically, petroglyphs, found throughout Nevada, Utah, and the Southwest, have proven difficult to decipher. Despite years of effort, scientists still don't know exactly what they mean. Some experts believe they have religious significance or are fertility symbols, while others think they relate to an activity such as hunting, since many seem to be found in places that were known as good spots for catching game. Or they could be nothing more than prehistoric Native American graffiti—doodles carved on a rock wall by bored Indians.

As for the thousand tombs, no amount of digging ever turned up a single buried body underneath those boulders. In the end, the site was not a North American Stonehenge or the Cradle of Civilization or a Nevada version of King Tut's burial chambers, as some had hoped.

Nevada may be a pretty interesting place—but it's no Garden of Eden.

CHAPTER 6

Haunted Carson City

No one ever has to dust the piano. *She* does it. It's said that every night she gives the fine, old black piano a thorough wipe, making sure the lid is nice and shiny and the ivory keys are dust free. No one ever sees her doing her chores, but the next day they see the results. No one seems to know why she does it. Perhaps she can't live with a dirty parlor or it just kills her to see a dusty piano. But who can tell since she's a ghost, said to reside in the historic Edwards House at 204 Minnesota Street in Carson City.

According to local legend, she is the spirit of a former housekeeper and nanny, Mrs. Maria Anderson, who apparently still can't abide a dirty house. Her favorite piece of furniture was the piano, which had been shipped around the Cape to Carson City. Various owners and tenants of the two-story, sandstone Victorian, which was built in 1883, have found that the musical instrument is the focus of most of her ectoplasmic cleaning: It never needs wiping or polishing no matter how much dust collects in the rest of the house. Additionally, several people have reported seeing a woman

RICHARD MORENO

The Nevada Governor's Mansion in Carson City is home to a mysterious clock and the ghost of a young girl.

sitting in the home's big bay windows—just as Mrs. Anderson loved to do when she was alive.

Other versions of the tale claim that the fastidious ghost is none other than Viola Edwards, wife of the home's original owner, Thomas J. Edwards, who appears at night to do a bit of light housecleaning. Calling that story into question is the fact that Mrs. Edwards died in 1877—five years before the home was built. Another longstanding rumor is that Thomas Edwards, who was the Ormsby County (which was consolidated into the combined city-county of Carson City in 1969) clerk from 1868 to 1877, used unpaid prison labor to build the house and, when it was discovered, was forced to resign his post. The story is not true, however, as Edwards was no longer the county clerk by the time the house was built.

In the 1990s, the Edwards House ghost story had become so well known that when the place was put up for sale, the owners listed it as "WESTSIDE VICTORIAN. Large lot zoned for residential/office and could be B&B, 4 bedrooms, wonderful parlours and living room, plus attached separate apartment. Piano and ghost included!"

Of course, the Edwards House isn't the Capital City's only haunted abode. Perhaps the most famous is the Nevada Governor's Mansion at 600 Mountain Street, where visitors and residents claim to have seen and heard a number of mysterious and unexplainable things. Over the years, mansion staff members have reported seeing a little girl dressed in a flowing white dress wandering the upstairs hallways. According to some, the girl is the ghost of June Dickerson, the only child ever born in the mansion (in 1909).

Additionally, a few guests and staff claim to have heard whispering and the low murmur of conversation in rooms—only to find no one there. There have also been tales about mysterious cold spots in various parts of the sprawling 23-room, Classical Revival–style mansion, which was completed in 1909, as well as that old ghostly standby: mysterious slamming doors.

Perhaps the most famous ghost story related to the mansion involves an antique grandfather clock that is said to contain a ghost. The clock is a classic, wind-up George Fowler clock, believed to be about 275 years old. House staff members aren't exactly sure how the old clock made its way into the mansion, but it has been there for decades. The clock didn't work for many years; it was repaired in 2007 by local horologists (clock makers). Over the years, mansion staffers have reported a number of odd experiences near the clock, including a cool breeze that doesn't seem to have a source. Helen Weimer, the mansion's coordinator from 1991 to 2010, told the *Nevada Appeal* newspaper that over the years, she has heard the stories about the mansion being haunted as well as at least a few unexplained noises. "People see a woman in a white gown or dress, walking around the mansion. Sometimes the doors of the clock will come open without a wind or anything," she told the paper. "One day I put the lights on and went on the outside balcony, and there was nothing there but a piece of very old cloth, old and yellow. And of all things, an old rusty jar lid with it.

"But the door to the clock opens regularly, then slams shut. It's really strange."

One mansion guest said she was kept awake by a late-night conversation that filtered through the walls only to discover that the woman in the next room had retired early and had not turned on either a radio or television set that evening. On a different occasion, a man cleaning the mansion library climbed a ladder to dust the books on the upper shelves and suddenly felt the temperature drop to near freezing—despite the fact it was a hot summer day and, at the time, the mansion did not have air-conditioning. The man ran frightened from the room and refused to return to his work. No word on whether anyone has dusted those books since.

Another allegedly haunted historic house is the Sears-Ferris House at 311 West Third Street. The modest two-story, wood-framed home was originally built by Mary and Gregory Sears in 1863, but was sold five years later to George Washington Gale Ferris Sr., a local horticulturist. Ferris's son, G. W. G. Ferris Jr., who grew up in the house, later invented the Ferris wheel for the Chicago World's Fair in 1893.

The first reported ghostly incident at the house is said to have happened in the early 1900s during a lavish wedding reception. Several guests at the party asked the bride's father the identity of a second woman dressed as a bride, who was standing by a back gate. The man said his daughter had been the only bride at the wedding, but the guests insisted they'd not only seen but also spoken to a second woman in a wedding dress. Later, it was discovered that there had been another wedding at the house many years before. Apparently, the ghost of the earlier bride had returned to the house to watch over the proceedings.

The Sears-Ferris House has also had reports of unexpected smells—for instance, fragrant men's cologne—as well as claims by residents that they were being watched. Supposedly, George Washington Gale Ferris Sr., who sold the house to his daughter in 1881, is said to have splashed on strong cologne after shaving.

Yet another home with a spirit is said to be the historic Bliss Mansion, a sprawling, three-story, nearly 8,000-square-foot Victorian Italianate–style home constructed in 1879. According to Dennis William Hauck, author of *The National Directory of Haunted Places*, the 21-room Bliss place, which once boasted its own ballroom, is said to have been erected atop an 1860s graveyard by Lake Tahoe lumber baron Duane L. Bliss. Some believe that ghosts of the exhumed and reburied pioneers have returned to the site and still wander the grounds.

Another spooky setting is the former home of Carson City founder Abraham Curry. According to Dennis Hauck, Curry has been seen wandering the rooms of the sandstone structure, which was finished in about 1871. Designed and constructed by Curry, who also built the US Mint and several other early Carson City buildings, the home at 406 North Nevada Street has five brick chimneys and originally boasted an octagonal cupola and five-bay porch (removed in the 1930s). Curry only lived in the home for about two years before dying at the age of fifty-eight.

Hauck claims that Curry's ghost has been seen gliding from room-to-room searching for his wife, Mary, who lived in the house until 1912, when she died at ninety-four. Despite being involved in the development of Carson City, Curry wasn't a very good business-man. In 1854, when he originally traveled west in search of gold, he had left his wife behind in his native state of New York. It took him until 1859 to earn enough money to send for her and his children. He built a fine home for his family but died in debt; his widow had to file a homestead notice to prevent the house from being taken from her. Because she had no way to make a living, Mary Curry was supported by two of her daughters for the last four decades of her life. It's said Curry returns to the house because he is haunted by the fact he left his family, and his wife in particular, destitute.

Curry's spirit is also said to haunt a second Carson City locale, the former US Mint building that he constructed in 1869–70. Hauck claims that Curry, who served as the Mint's director during its first few years, has been seen trolling the hallways of the old building, which is now home to the Nevada State Museum.

The Brewery Arts Center, formerly the Carson City Brewing Company, also boasts a good ghost story. Built in 1864, the two-story brick structure on the corner of King and North Division

Streets was the home of the brewing operations of Nevada's first brewery, with products that included Tahoe Beer. During prohibition, the company branched into "near-beer" (a low-alcohol alternative to beer) as well as soft drinks, mineral water, and ice. In the late 1940s, the brewery folded because it was unable to compete with the growing strength of national beer brands. From 1950 to 1974, the building housed the local newspaper, the *Nevada Appeal*. Since 1976, the nonprofit Brewery Arts Center has owned the building, which is used for classes, art shows, theater performances, and plays. Dennis Hauck says members of the latter groups have reported hearing a "pleasant, discarnate" voice, which makes suggestions regarding the various theatrical productions and reminds visitors to close doors and extinguish lights. In other words, it's a darned polite ghost.

The capital city's final haunted habitat is said to be the area of the city that once housed a thriving red-light district. According to city records, this sector encompassed the neighborhood roughly bordered by Nevada Street on the west, Fifth Street to the south, Second Street to the north, and Carson Street to the east. In 1875, the Carson City Board of Trustees passed an ordinance creating such a zone, which remained on the books into the early twentieth century.

In 1880, a bizarre spat involving a man, the prostitute who loved him, and another prostitute—who loved her—resulted in one of the women being viciously murdered. According to author Alton Pryor, who chronicled various Old West "cribs" in his book *The Bawdy House Girls: A Look at the Brothels of the Old West*, the episode involved a prostitute named Timber Kate, who made a living performing live sex acts with her female lover, Bella Rawhide, on stages in seedy honky-tonk joints throughout Nevada, Washington, and Wyoming.

Rawhide, however, became interested in a man named Tug Daniels and ran off with him, leaving behind a heartbroken Kate. According to Pryor, the partner-less Kate found the only way to make a living was to dress as a man in white tights and to lift weights—then shock the crowd by revealing her true gender during a slow strip act at the end. One day, however, when she was performing in the Bee Hive brothel in Carson City, she spotted Rawhide and Daniels in the audience. There was a loud argument that culminated in Daniels pulling his knife and slashing Kate, according to Pryor, "from her crotch to her navel." She fell to the ground and quickly bled to death. Daniels fled the scene of the crime and managed to disappear; he was never heard from again. Perhaps consumed with guilt, Rawhide killed herself two years later by downing a bottle of cleaning fluid. According to Dennis Hauck, Timber Kate returns to the scene of her violent demise. He reports that her ghost has been seen wandering the streets of the old red-light district searching for her lover.

CHAPTER 7

The Great Carson City Stagecoach Robbery

It was a near-perfect holdup. Sometime in the late 1860s or early 1870s, a Wells Fargo stagecoach was transporting more than $60,000 in gold bullion from the Comstock region's fabulous mines to the new US Mint in Carson City, where it was to be melted down and stamped into gold coins. The first three-quarters of the 13-mile trip had been uneventful as the stage bounced along on the rutted dirt road between Virginia City and Carson City. The driver and his armed companion visibly relaxed when they reached the point on the trip where they could see ahead to the trees and buildings of Carson City.

That's when the four robbers struck. After the stage passed through the small settlement of Empire, only a few miles east of Carson City, the quartet of armed men leaped out of the bushes with their guns blazing. They managed to stop the coach and demand that the driver and his guard throw down their weapons and toss down the strongbox filled with gold bullion. After quickly

This 1911 re-creation of a stagecoach robbery is about as authentic as the oft-told tales of a daring holdup that allegedly occurred near Carson City in the late 1860s or early 1870s.

collecting the loot, the outlaws sent the stage on its way with the driver and his guard unharmed.

Once the driver and his guard reached Carson City, word spread about the robbery and a posse was quickly formed to go after the thieves. They saddled up, raced out of town and, a few miles west of town, caught up to the outlaws. Seeing the lawmen closing fast, the robbers opened fire and soon bullets were flying in all directions. Minutes after the gunfight had started, it was over. Three of the highwaymen were killed and a fourth was captured.

The man in custody was Manuel Gonzales (also simply called the Mexican in some accounts). But while the local sheriff and his posse had clearly nabbed the culprits, they could not find the loot. A search of the trail and surrounding areas yielded no clues as to what could have happened to the 300 pounds of gold bullion. After Gonzales was safely locked in the local jail, he was questioned about the whereabouts of the stolen gold. But he wouldn't talk.

Gonzales was convicted and sentenced to 20 years in the Nevada State Prison in Carson City. And still he wouldn't talk. In fact, the only thing he revealed to other prisoners was that he could see the location of the hidden treasure from his prison window. Eight years into his sentence, Gonzales grew ill with consumption and was pardoned by the governor. The legal authorities kept a close eye on the ailing ex-convict, believing that eventually he would try to dig up his hidden gold cache. For several months, he made no effort to try to reclaim his blood prize.

As he went about his daily life, Gonzales befriended a local butcher, known as the Old Dutchman. The meat cutter was curious about the missing bullion and began pestering the dying outlaw, urging him to share his secret. Finally, Gonzales relented and agreed to show his friend where he and his partners had stashed their treasure. Unfortunately, Gonzales never got the chance to follow through. As the two walked to the site where the bullion was buried, Gonzales suddenly clutched his chest and sat down. Within a few minutes, he keeled over dead, having never talked.

Since that day, treasure hunters with metal detectors and other fortune seekers have scoured the hills west of Carson City, hoping to find and claim the gold, which would be worth considerably more in current dollars. One website reported that it's not unusual for Nevada State Prison guards to spend their weekends searching for the gold.

The robbery and subsequent quest for the stolen goods make a great story. Too bad none of it is true.

Over the years, former Nevada State archivist Guy Louis Rocha had heard and read about the robbery but wondered whether it was true. So he went to work trying to find out everything he could about this sensational crime, which seemed to be one of the West's biggest stagecoach holdups. He checked local and state newspaper archives, certain that a robbery this important and of this magnitude would be big news, but he found nothing. He called Wells Fargo and spoke to its official historian, Dr. Robert J. Chandler, who found no record of such a crime. "Papers nationwide would have carried the story," Dr. Chandler told him.

Rocha traced the origin of the story to a 1935 book of prison-related stories published by the former Nevada State Prison warden, Matt Penrose. Called *Pots O' Gold*, the book recounts a number of historic crime- and prison-related episodes including the death of outlaw Sam Brown, train robberies, and public executions. Plus, there is a chapter devoted to the Carson City stagecoach robbery.

"Can a story be just too good to be true? A much-told tale of a Carson City area stagecoach robbery in the late nineteenth century fails to hold up under scrutiny," Rocha wrote. "People still search for the loot somewhere in the vicinity of the old State Prison. The story, however, is pure invention."

Rocha also looked at the details of the crime—why would such a large amount of gold bullion be transported in a stagecoach to the US Mint in Carson, which didn't begin minting coins until early 1870, when the Virginia & Truckee Railroad, which ran between Virginia City and Carson City, was completed by January of that year? He also questioned the description of the bullion, noting that $60,000 in gold bullion would have to weigh about ten times more than 300 pounds. He also found no evidence that a Manuel Gonzales or any Hispanic male had ever been arrested or tried for a stagecoach robbery in or near Carson City and that no one by that name ever served time in the state prison.

Despite evidence to the contrary, however, there are those who insist the treasure is real and still out there. It's not unusual to spot folks with metal detectors traipsing around Prison Hill (directly east of the state prison in Carson City). Additionally, the website for *Coin World* magazine lists the Wells Fargo treasure from the Empire State near Carson City as one of the "Nevada treasures waiting to be found." In *Lost Gold and Silver Mines of the Southwest*, author Eugene L. Conrotto repeats much of the story concocted in the Penrose book but adds that it most likely happened in 1885. A similar tale appeared in a 1954 issue of *Desert Magazine*.

Interestingly, it appears that Penrose was not even the author of the book that bears his name and that birthed the whole saga of the Carson City robbery. Philip I. Earl, retired curator of history for the Nevada Historical Society, revealed in a 2005 *Nevada Magazine* article that *Pots O' Gold* was actually written by a notorious and gifted conman named John K. "Jack" Meredith, who was in prison at the time. Meredith was convicted of forgery in 1933 and sentenced to the state prison in Carson City. He had a lengthy rap sheet that included previous stints in jails in Montana, Wisconsin, and Missouri (for forgery), a term in the federal penitentiary at McNeil Island, Washington, for bootlegging, and he claimed to be wanted for other crimes in Idaho, Oregon, and Colorado.

Meredith, however, had a way with words. Within a short time, he became the head of the literacy program at the prison and began teaching other inmates how to read and write. He also edited a monthly inmate magazine, *The Rainbow*, for which he also contributed a regular column, and he apparently wrote *Pots O' Gold*, a 233-page collection of stories about the history of the state prison, the state's first gas execution in 1934, the story of the prehistoric sloth footprints found at the prison, and other tales, for the warden.

According to Earl, eager-to-please Meredith also became a bit of an expert in lifting fingerprints, making casts of footprints, and analyzing evidence. He earned the gratitude of a number of Nevada and California lawmen by offering his forensic expertise and detection skills to help them solve several crimes.

On May 17, 1937, Sheriff Orrin Brown of Alpine County, California, sought Meredith's help in looking for about $10,000 in stolen jewelry reportedly buried in a mine shaft. Meredith said he had overheard another convict talking about the jewelry and where it was hidden. Brown received permission to take Meredith with him to the mine site. The two ascended a steep mountainside, with Meredith eventually climbing ahead of the sheriff. From his higher perspective, Meredith yelled back to Brown that he could see an easier way to reach the mine and directed the sheriff to circle around the mountain to another trail.

As soon as Brown was out of his line of sight, Meredith scampered back to the car, where the sheriff had left his coat, wallet, and, most important, the keys to the vehicle. The convict started the car and made his escape. Earl wrote that Meredith's luck almost ran out when he managed to get the car stuck in sand a few miles from where he had fled Sheriff Brown. Fortunately for him, a sheep packer drove up and offered to help. Meredith concocted a story about how the sheriff had broken his leg on the mountain and he was driving to get help when he became stuck. The Good Samaritan agreed to drive Meredith to the closest garage, which was in Minden. There, Meredith repeated his tale of misfortune, which was so convincing that the garage owner offered Meredith the use of a new sedan with a full tank of gas.

It was more than eight months before authorities captured Meredith. In the interim, he traveled to Idaho (law enforcement officials had incorrectly assumed he would flee to Los Angeles, and they had centered their efforts there), where, in a display of remarkable chutzpah, he began cashing bad checks under the forged signature of William S. Harris, the prison's purchasing agent. It turned out that Meredith had planned his escape well and had lifted a book of state checks and a pad of state purchase-order forms.

From that point, Meredith crisscrossed the country—writing bad checks along the way—keeping one step ahead of John Law. In mid-June, his forged handiwork showed up in Ohio, and then a couple of weeks later in Seattle, Washington. A day later, he popped up in Indianapolis, and later that week was in Cedar Rapids, Iowa. In the following weeks, he tried to cash checks in Covington, Kentucky, and in Baltimore.

His jumping around from state to state quickly gained the attention of the FBI, who joined the hunt. According to Earl, the *Gardnerville Record-Courier* reported on July 2, 1937, "G-men are on his trail and sooner or later Meredith will be apprehended. In the meantime he is having a splendid vacation touring the country . . . and living off the fat of the land as a result of his ability to pass bum checks."

The chase finally ended on January 27, 1938, in New York City. Meredith tried to pull a complete chameleon job by presenting himself as Dr. Roy J. Griffith, retired professor of geography and journalism from the University of Notre Dame. Bank officials became suspicious and alerted authorities about his attempt to cash a forged check. Meredith was arrested and, after checking his fingerprints against the records, he was unmasked. Earl noted that the person most relieved at Meredith's capture was Harris, the state prison purchasing agent. He quoted Harris as saying, "It was getting so that I hardly dared to write one of my own checks."

Meredith was soon extradited to Nevada, where he was given his former prison number and tossed into solitary confinement for a month. It appears he was a model prisoner during the next four years, as he was paroled on October 4, 1942. But old habits die hard, and a few months later he was back to trying to pass bad checks in Arizona—and there were reports that he may also have been doing so in Georgia, Tennessee, Washington, and Indiana. He was arrested again in June 1944 and sentenced to twenty-three years in the federal penitentiary in Atlanta. In August 1958, at the age of sixty-two, he was given his conditional release from prison. This time, he may have learned his lesson because he was never heard from again.

In perhaps the biggest irony, Meredith's ghost-written work, *Pots O' Gold*, is now considered a rare Nevada book. When copies do turn up on the antiquarian book market, they command as much as several hundred dollars each. In his authoritative *Nevada: An Annotated Bibliography*, author Stanley W. Paher describes it as "a choice Nevadiana item."

Not bad for a book by a fake author about a fake crime.

CHAPTER 8

The First Train Robbery
in the Far West

John Chapman had it all figured out but he wanted to be certain the rest of the crew knew their roles. He and several of his friends had pulled off a number of smaller jobs, mostly involving Wells Fargo stagecoaches traveling through Washoe and Storey Counties, but this was much bigger. Chapman, along with A. J. "Jack" Davis, John Squiers, R. A. "Sol" Jones, Chat Roberts, John Gilchrist, Tilton Cockerell, and E. B. Parsons, were going to rob a Central Pacific Railroad train of its bounty of gold coins, silver bars, and paper money.

At the time, train robberies were something new in America. The first recorded peacetime theft of a moving train in the United States had occurred on October 6, 1866, when members of the Reno Brothers Gang boarded an Ohio & Mississippi Railroad train near Seymour, Indiana. According to some reports, they managed to break into one safe containing about $16,000 and tossed a second one off the train. The gang, which also robbed banks and courthouses, was so pleased by the success of its train caper that it robbed another one in December 1867 and a third in July 1868. The gang's exploits, however, quickly attracted the attention of the Pinkerton National Detective Agency, which the railroad hired to catch the outlaws. By mid-1868, Pinkerton agents had tracked down and captured every member of the gang. An interesting post-script is that only one member of the gang, John Reno, avoided being lynched (he served ten years in prison). The rest were taken from jail by armed vigilantes and executed.

Of course, none of this mattered to Chapman and his co-conspirators. They had concocted a simple but elegant plan. He went over the plan again with the others. He would travel to San Francisco and select a train heading east through Reno, Nevada, that would be brimming with gold, silver, and money. Once he had chosen, he would send a coded telegram to Jones, who would convey the message to Davis and the others. When the train stopped to replenish its water and wood in the small lumber town of Verdi, west of Reno, gang members would sneak onto the train, overpower the conductor, break into the express car, loot the safe, and escape. Chapman and the others also figured that the train would be lightly guarded since the Central Pacific Railroad had only completed construction of a transcontinental rail line in May 1869—and no Far West train had ever been robbed before.

Most of the gang members brought something to the table: The studious Chapman had helped to develop the plan; a for-mer mining supervisor, Davis, was affable but tough; Squiers was the veteran bandit, someone who had previously robbed several stagecoaches; Parsons was a professional gambler, who

Washoe County Undersheriff James H. Kinkead

understood playing for high stakes; and Cockerell was an ex-army officer who knew his way around firearms. Gilchrist, Roberts, and Jones were inexperienced but needed to provide the necessary backup and muscle.

On the evening of November 4, 1870, Chapman, who was a Sunday school teacher, sent the message: "Send me $60 tonight without fail," signed by "J. Enrique." Jones immediately recognized the meaning—the next train leaving the San Francisco area would be carrying about $60,000 in coins, bars, and cash, and it was the one to rob. And, in fact, Central Pacific Railroad Locomotive No. 1 did depart from Oakland late that night with an express car containing $41,600 in gold coins, $8,800 in silver bars, and many more thousands of dollars in paper money.

The gang assembled in an abandoned mine shaft near Hunter's Crossing (a few miles east of Verdi) according to plan, but started to grow anxious when the train didn't appear on schedule. A freight wreck near Truckee, California, delayed it for more than an hour. Finally, just as they were starting to question whether they should try another time, they spotted the train chugging through the light snow flurries as it crossed into Nevada. A little after midnight, it stopped in Verdi to take on water and to reload the tender with split wood logs. As the train began to pick up speed and head to Reno, five armed men, all wearing masks and linen dusters, hopped onto the moving train. Davis and another man crawled over the woodpile and dropped into the engine room. With pistols pointed at the engineer and fireman, they ordered them to continue heading east. Meanwhile, the other three bandits scampered to the express car.

About a half mile east of Verdi, Davis prompted the engineer to whistle "down brakes," which was a signal to the other three robbers to pull the coupling-pin and separate the rest of the train from the express car, mail car, and locomotive. Washoe County Undersheriff James H. Kinkead later wrote that as soon as this was done, Davis told the engineer to speed up, which quickly created distance between the outlaws and any railroad employees in the cars that were set adrift.

"The robbers then speeded down the grade with this part of the train, leaving the other cars at a standstill. The engineer, realizing what was being done, at first refused to pull out, but the muzzle of a pistol against his temple caused him to obey orders," Kinkead wrote.

About 5 miles from Reno, the train came to a stop because of an obstruction placed on the track by the robbers. Once the train had stopped moving, the three bandits at the express car ordered the inside guard, Frank Minch, to open the door. With a sawed-off shotgun pointed at his face, Minch surrendered without incident and was made to sit in a corner. The gold coins were stacked in the car in Wells Fargo sacks. The three men tossed the bags from a side door into the surrounding thick brush. Kinkead reported that one of the thieves thanked Minch for not giving them any trouble and said he was glad he didn't have to shoot him. At this point, the robbers jumped from the train and disappeared into the night.

Meanwhile, momentum carried the unconnected sections of the train east until they caught up with the stalled locomotive, mail car, and express car. The engineer and fireman quickly began clearing the track of obstructions and—with all the train cars reconnected—raced toward Reno to alert railroad officials and law enforcement authorities about the holdup. Early the next morning, Washoe County Sheriff Charley Pegg and Kinkead learned about the robbery and received a telegram from C. C. Pendergast, the Wells Fargo agent in Virginia City, Nevada, who wrote, "Train robbed between Truckee and Verdi; robbers gone south." Hoping for a quick return of its stolen money and metal, railroad officials joined with the Wells Fargo Express Company as well as county and state authorities to post rewards that totaled some $30,000.

The two lawmen quickly climbed on their horses and set out for the mountains, assuming, according to Kinkead, that the outlaws would take a route south through Washoe Valley to either Carson City or Virginia City. But after spending a day looking for tracks that weren't there, they concluded that Pendergast's message had been wrong and returned to Reno. The next day, they headed to the scene of the crime, east of Verdi, where they discovered a clue—a boot print that was different from the others.

"It was made by a boot having a very small heel, such as the dudes and the gamblers wore in those days and our wives and daughters wear now," Kinkead wrote. "No laboring man or railroad employee ever wore that boot, and it was too soon after the robbery for the curious to have visited the ground."

Kinkead traced the tracks in each direction from the scene of the crime—in an attempt to confuse any pursuers, the robbers walked on the railroad ties for some distance before stepping back onto the ground—and found that about a mile to the west, the small boot print and two larger imprints reappeared in the snow and headed north. He followed them along Dog Valley Creek and over Dog Valley Hill into California's Sardine Valley.

The tracks led to a small inn and restaurant called the Sardine Valley House. The woman who owned the establishment told Kinkead that three strangers had spent the previous night in her place but two had departed early in the morning. The third one, however, had been taken to the Truckee jail by a group of local hunters who had learned of the robbery and determined he was involved when he suspiciously tried to slip away. Apparently, he had seen them with their weapons and assumed they were lawmen. In its November 11, 1870, edition, Virginia City's *Territorial Enterprise* newspaper reported that the man had "appeared excited [after hearing the hunters talk about the robbery] and said he must go out. He went back to the privy and his manner was so strange that parties followed him and they found six $20 pieces soon after he left."

The woman also provided Kinkead with detailed descriptions of the other two men. Most interesting to the undersheriff was the fact that one of the men wore "gambler's boots." From the woman's description Kinkead quickly surmised that the other man might be John Squiers, a notorious local highwayman who had been robbing Storey County stagecoaches for many years but who had never been captured. Kinkead also knew that Squiers had a brother who was a law-abiding blacksmith in Sierra Valley, which was north.

After resting his horse, Kinkead continued in pursuit of the two men. In his record of events, he wrote that it was after 10 p.m. and snow was falling. Since he wasn't familiar with the way to Sierra Valley, he persuaded a ten-year-old boy to guide him at least part of the way (for $10). At about midnight, the undersheriff arrived in the town of Loyalton in the Sierra Valley. He stopped at the only hotel in town and woke the landlord to ask if he had rented a room to any "strange guests." The landlord replied that there was one fellow from out of town, although he didn't seem all that strange nor did he fit the description provided by the undersheriff.

Kinkead still wanted to check out the man, so the landlord gave him a candle and pointed him in the direction of Room 14.

The undersheriff quietly crept down the hallway to the room. When he reached it, he found that the door was slightly ajar. The hotel had just been built and was unpainted, and the damp weather caused the doors to swell and fail to shut tightly enough to lock. Kinkead gently pushed open the door. The man was sleeping soundly. Using the candle for illumination, the lawman took a quick look around. Then, he stopped. There, lying on the floor next to the bed was a boot with a very distinctive, small heel. A gambler's boot. Kinkead searched the room for a weapon and found a six-shooter tucked under the sleeping man's pillow. He checked the man's clothing pockets and found "further evidence to connect him with the robbery," according to Kinkead.

Finished with his impromptu investigation, Kinkead shook the man awake. The man jumped out of bed "like a wild animal" and reached for his gun. Meanwhile, Kinkead kept his Henry rifle trained on the man and calmly commanded him to get dressed. Realizing he had little bargaining power, the man did as he was told and marched ahead of Kinkead as the undersheriff led him out of the hotel and down the street to the saloon, where he was bound and placed under armed guard by local authorities. The man in the small-heeled boots was the Virginia City gambler, E. B. Parsons.

After securing Parsons, Kinkead went in search of Squiers. He was given directions to Joe Squiers's (John's brother) house and, after finding it, decided to wait until daylight to see who might emerge. As the sun rose, a man with a bucket opened the door and walked to a barn to do the morning milking. The undersheriff had once arrested John Squiers, and he knew the man in the barn wasn't the outlaw. The door to the house was left slightly open, so Kinkead entered the residence. He quietly searched the rooms in the house until he found John Squiers sleeping soundly. Just as he was able to do with Parsons, he confiscated the slumbering man's firearm, and then collected his boots and clothes. He roused the sleeping Squiers with the barrel of his rifle and ordered him to put on his clothing.

As Kinkead led Squiers from the house, the man in the barn emerged. Squiers yelled that he was being robbed, which awoke everyone in the house. As Squiers's friends and relatives gathered around the undersheriff and his prisoner, Kinkead told them that he was a lawman who was arresting Squiers on suspicion of robbing a Central Pacific Railroad train. The wily Squiers protested that Kinkead's legal authority only extended to the Nevada state line and he should be freed. The crowd began to murmur that Squiers made a good point. However, before things could turn ugly, Kinkead slowly but firmly pushed his prisoner into a wagon containing Parsons, which was parked behind the saloon. With an eye on the crowd, he immediately set off for Truckee. Once there, he jailed Squiers and Parsons with the man brought in by the hunters, who turned out to be John Gilchrist.

Kinkead telegraphed Nevada's Governor Henry G. Blasdel and requested that the governor formally ask California's governor, Henry Haight, for permission to extradite the prisoners back to the Silver State. The following day, approval was granted and the prisoners were placed—ironically—on the next Central Pacific Railroad train to Reno. During the hours that Kinkead and the prisoners were in Truckee, the undersheriff had kept Gilchrist, who was a miner by trade, separated from the other two hard cases. He questioned him repeatedly, telling him that he wasn't sure how long he could protect him from the angry mob that had formed outside the jail. The frightened Gilchrist finally cracked and signed a full confession before a notary public, providing names of every person involved in the crime.

After sweating Gilchrist, Kinkead sent a telegraph message to the Wells Fargo office in Virginia City, directing authorities to immediately arrest Jack Davis. He sent a second telegram to Reno, instructing his office to pick up Chapman, Jones, Roberts, and Cockerell. That same day, Virginia City police captured Davis while Jones, Roberts, and Cockerell were hunted down and arrested in Long Valley, located northwest of Reno. Chapman had not yet returned from San Francisco but was taken into custody the following day as soon as he stepped off the train. The entire gang had been rounded up in less than four days following the robbery.

As for the loot, the talkative Gilchrist led officers to a tunnel containing most of the gold, silver bars, and paper money. He said the money was to have remained hidden until the heat died down, and then the members would divvy up the spoils and go their separate ways. According to most accounts, authorities recovered all but 150 gold coins.

Typical of the frontier justice of the times, a grand jury quickly indicted the eight suspects, who went to trial in December 1870, a little more than a month after the robbery. Kinkead wrote that the trial was a "memorable one in the criminal annals of Nevada." Chapman's attorney, Judge Thomas E. Haydon of Reno, argued that his client could not be charged with the crime in Nevada because he had been in San Francisco on the day it was committed. Additionally, he said the state of Nevada had no jurisdiction in the case unless it could prove that Chapman was part of a conspiracy that had been concocted in Nevada.

In response, attorneys for the state and county produced Gilchrist and Roberts, who testified that Chapman had helped plan the robbery during a clandestine meeting at Roberts's ranch in Nevada. Jones, who also agreed to help the prosecution in return for a lighter sentence, testified that Chapman had sent the coded message and translated it for the court. While Chapman tried to deny even sending the coded telegram, a Western Union operator in San Francisco positively identified him as J. Enrique, the author of the message.

Eventually, all the defendants were found guilty of the robbery. Gilchrist and Roberts were allowed to go free in return for their testimony against the others while Jones received a five-year sentence in the Nevada State Prison. Squiers, who had resisted arrest, received the harshest sentence—twenty-three years—while the man who planned the crime, Chapman, was given twenty years. Cockerell received twenty-two years while Parsons got eighteen years and Davis earned ten years.

"Chapman and Squiers conceived the idea of holding up a railroad train," Kinkead concluded. "It was a remarkably well-concocted plan, and all the details were worked out to perfection, the only mistake being in the selection of the men. They did not need Gilchrist and Jones, who were novices in the business and gave up everything they knew under pressure of the sweatbox."

There are a couple of interesting postscripts to the story. In September 1871, four of the unsuccessful train robbers, Chapman, Cockerell, Parsons, and Squiers, joined in a violent prison break during which several guards were seriously injured or killed and warden Frank Denver was tied up. Newspaper reports from the time indicated that twenty-nine prisoners escaped, although most were recaptured within days of the break.

During the commotion, Davis elected not to join the others and defended some of the guards from being harmed by the rampaging inmates. For his assistance, Davis's sentence was reduced to five years. Despite his apparent change of heart, within a year after being released from prison Davis was back to robbing stagecoaches. In September 1877, Davis and two confederates, Bob Hamilton and Thomas Lauria, attempted to rob one heading from Eureka to Tybo. Unknown to the three, the coach contained two armed messengers. When the three masked men stepped in front of the stage, the two opened fire with double-barreled shotguns. Davis took a cloud of buckshot in the chest and was killed immediately. The other two escaped but were quickly captured and eventually sentenced to fourteen years in the state prison.

Another story that has floated around for years is that the train robbery was actually planned and executed by the notorious outlaws Butch Cassidy and the Sundance Kid. Nothing in the records, however, indicates the involvement of either of the two desperadoes or any members of their infamous Wild Bunch gang.

It is true, however, that the same Central Pacific Railroad Locomotive No. 1, that was robbed near Verdi on November 5, 1870, was again held up less than a day later. According to historian Howard Hickson, the second robbery took place about twenty hours after the first in far northeastern Nevada, near the rail town of Toana. Four thieves—who had no affiliation with the Chapman-Davis gang—hopped aboard the train in the Pequop Mountains, located a few miles west of Toana. They made their way to the express car, which had just taken on thousands of dollars during a stop in Elko.

Unfortunately for the outlaws, the Wells Fargo clerk in the car had not had time to put all the money in the safe, so when the gang began pounding on the door to be let inside, he quietly hid much of it in piles of other freight, then blew out his lamp. When the robbers finally gained entry into the dark car, they demanded he open the safe, which he did. The crooks found about $3,100, which they grabbed, but never suspected that considerably more cash was tucked away in the rest of the car.

The four jumped off the train and disappeared. Hickson has written that Elko County lawmen followed several false leads before finally arresting three men—Daniel Taylor, Daniel Baker, and Leander Morton—on November 30, 1870, for robbing the train. The identity of the fourth member of the group was never revealed nor was anyone ever arrested. Hickson said the three men were convicted of the crime in January 1871 and sentenced to thirty years each. In another amazing coincidence, Morton was the ringleader during the Nevada State Prison breakout later that year. He led a group of escaped convicts that tried to flee to the Death Valley area to hide until the spring but encountered a posse in Long Valley (south of Mammoth Lakes) that shot and killed several of the renegade inmates. Morton was captured and hanged (reportedly because the reward money was so little that it wasn't worth the effort to take him back to Carson City).

And what about the 150 $20 gold coins? Former Nevada archivist Guy Louis Rocha notes that "people still hunt in the vicinity of the robbery for the 150 missing gold coins now estimated to be worth over $500,000." So the next time you're in Reno hoping to strike it rich, ignore the blackjack tables and one-armed bandits and head west to a place called Hunter's Crossing. There just might be gold in them there hills.

CHAPTER 9

The Mystery of the Lost City

The year was 1150. A thriving community of perhaps several thousand people stretched over some twenty-five miles along the banks of the Virgin and Muddy Rivers in southeastern Nevada's Moapa Valley. These people, now called the Puebloans, harvested crops, including corn, cotton, beans, and squash, and built sturdy stone, wood, and adobe dwellings—some quite large and interconnected with dozens of rooms. They mined salt and dug ditches to irrigate their fields. They made pottery decorated with bold designs and patterns on red, black, and white backgrounds.

These early pre-Nevadans used cotton to weave blankets and clothing, and traded with other tribes, or so it appears because of the presence of shell and turquoise pendants as well as stone and shell beads, which are not indigenous to southern Nevada. They also had leisure time, as evidenced from the flat bone dice, dolls, and toy dishes that have been unearthed, and they frequently painted themselves for special ceremonies.

But then they disappeared.

Sometime in the twelfth century, the Puebloans abandoned their expansive settlement with its hundreds of dwellings, cultivated fields, and developed mines, which former Nevada governor James Scrugham, himself an amateur historian and archaeologist, named Pueblo Grande de Nevada, or Grand House of Nevada, and the media, fascinated with tales of long-forgotten civilizations, called the Lost City. Archaeologist Mark R. Harrington, who excavated the region in the 1920s and 1930s at Scrugham's request, wrote in 1935, "What the reasons were for this decline we do not know ... what became of the Pueblos who had absorbed the Basketmakers, nobody knows. It is thought that they worked their way eastward and joined with other related tribes to become the ancestors of the present Hopi or other Pueblo Indians."

It's believed that the first people to settle in the valleys around the Muddy and Virgin Rivers, which are located about 60 miles northeast of Las Vegas, arrived in about 300 BC. These first residents may have shared a language or culture with neighboring Southwestern Indians and had similar tools and crafts. These prehistoric people, often referred to as the Anasazi, used spears and the *atlatl* (a kind of dart-throwing device) to hunt as well as crooked, flat clubs and flint knives. They also crafted bags woven of native hemp and made extraordinarily fine baskets: In fact, the other name commonly used to describe them is the Basketmakers. Archaeologists have also found corncobs and husks, indicating they knew how to grow crops.

The Basketmakers resided in underground pit houses that were 10 to 15 feet in diameter and about 6 feet deep. They also created a type of writing, called petroglyphs, which included patterns,

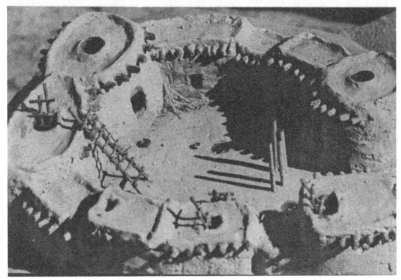

The excavation of the mysterious prehistoric Lost City in Southern Nevada was spotlighted in the March 1946 issue of *The Nevada Magazine* (not related to the current *Nevada Magazine*).

stick figures, animal shapes, and other designs carved into boulders and rock walls. Although the meaning of the rock writings died with these early settlers, some scientists today believe that the etchings may have been spiritual in nature, perhaps related to shamanism or a vision quest.

Harrington noted, "In no case can Nevada 'rock-writings' be read as a connected story, as some people imagine. Some picture a single event, others are prayers for good hunting, directions for finding water, maps, religious symbols, personal signatures, even haphazard scrawls made for amusement while passing the hot midday hours in the shadow of the rock."

Petroglyphs from this period have been found throughout southern Nevada, but most prominently at Atlatl Rock in the Valley of Fire State Park, located near the site of the Lost City. There, visitors can still find humanlike stick figures as well as carvings of bighorn sheep, handprints, snakes, circles, and what is considered one of the finest representations of an atlatl.

Archaeologists have divided the Basketmakers into an early and a late period, with the latter producing more elaborate types of pottery and having a far more sophisticated farming culture. They also knew how to use bows and arrows to hunt. Their dwellings also evolved, moving away from being completely underground to being partially aboveground—sort of an early split-level home. The roofs were dome-shaped and made with willows and rushes and then covered with mud. As with the homes of the earlier Basketmakers, the entrance remained through the roof, with residents using a ladder to climb into the house. The late Basketmakers grew corn and other grains, which were crushed using a grooved stone slab called a metate.

For unknown reasons, the Pueblo people replaced the Basketmakers in about AD 500 or 600. Historians often refer to this group as the First Stage Pueblos or Pueblo II people. It's not known whether the Basketmakers were conquered by the Pueblos, merged with them peacefully, or simply moved on. According to archaeologists, among the more significant differences between the two cultures were their dwellings. The Puebloans built even more sophisticated adobe structures: In this case, they were constructed with logs covered with adobe mud, and were largely above the ground. Unlike the early Basketmaker houses, which were entered through the ceiling, these homes had openings in the side wall. Additionally, the pottery created by the Puebloans incorporated bold black designs and patterns on a white background, while the earlier Basketmaker pottery had more delicate black lines and dots on a gray background.

Over time, the Pueblo people evolved into the culture that developed the Lost City. These later Puebloans constructed far grander and elaborate communities. Houses, which now were entirely aboveground, contained dozens of rooms and usually surrounded a circular or horseshoe-shaped courtyard. The biggest of these dwellings that has been found had almost one hundred separate rooms. The Lost City period also saw the introduction of irrigation techniques to water crops, digging sticks to work in the gardens, and a wider variety of crops including beans, squash, gourds, and cotton. Lost City Puebloans also developed mining to obtain rock salt, turquoise, and minerals that could be used to make paint and color pottery.

Lost City crafts were also different and included pottery that was decorated with more elaborate and more carefully executed lines. The types of pots now encompassed water jars, pitchers, and different sizes of bowls and cooking containers—all of which were sometimes painted red as well as black, white, and gray. The late Puebloans had also learned how to weave cotton into blankets, women's dresses, and breeches for men.

But then something happened to the Lost City Pueblo people, who seemed to just vanish. Many scientists speculate that a prolonged drought was the most likely culprit for the decline of the Lost City, but no one can be sure. Harrington speculated that "possibly a succession of dry years drove many of the people away or a series of floods buried their fields with gravel. We suspect strongly that nomadic wild tribes had something to do with it, because the last Pueblo settlements in the Moapa Valley, which will probably date around AD 800, were placed on mesa tops and in other situations easy of defense."

Evidence indicates that the Southern Paiutes and Shoshone, whose descendants still live in Moapa Valley and southern Nevada, eventually replaced the Lost City people. Harrington described the latecomers as a seminomadic people who learned at least some of the skills of the earlier residents. He noted that the early Southern Paiutes made crude pottery and had some basic knowledge of agriculture while their brethren to the north (Northern Paiutes and Northern Shoshone), who live in the parts of the state where the Puebloans never resided, had no tradition of either.

Interestingly, the first mention of the ruins of the Lost City appeared in Jedediah Smith's account of exploring the area in 1826–27. While Smith's report to General William Clark (of Lewis and Clark fame) largely focused on waterways and mountain ranges, he casually mentioned discovering salt caves on the banks of the Virgin River in which he found stone tools. It would be nearly a century before anyone else paid much attention to those caves.

By the early 1920s, John and Fay Perkins, two brothers who grew up in Overton, had wandered the banks of the Muddy and Virgin Rivers, exploring the salt caves and other ancient Indian ruins. In 1924, Fay sent a package containing prehistoric Indian artifacts to Nevada governor James Scrugham, a former state engineer and a man fascinated by Nevada's rich history. In a note, Perkins explained that he and his brother, descendants of Mormon pioneers, had found the items—along with plenty more—along the Muddy River. Scrugham was intrigued and contacted Harrington, who was excavating the Lovelock Cave (90 miles east of Reno) at the time. Harrington was curious about what exactly the Perkins brothers had discovered and agreed to join the governor in checking out the site.

Journalist K. J. Evans later reported that when Harrington arrived at the site, he was surprised to find that not only the governor was there but also a handful of newspaper and magazine reporters, film crews, and a large crowd of people. "To raise money for the project—and to get favorable publicity for his state—Scrugham threw a pageant, depicting the valley's prehistory and history. It was held May 23, 1925, at the end of the digging season. A replica of a Pueblo was constructed for a stage," Evans wrote.

After Scrugham and Harrington were shown what the Perkinses had uncovered, they became excited. Scrugham immediately asked Harrington's benefactor, George Gustav Heye, head of the Museum of the American Indian, to authorize an excavation under the archaeologist's direction. To assist the archaeologist, the governor assigned state equipment, vehicles, and workers to help with the dig and successfully petitioned the Smithsonian and the Carnegie institutions for additional funds.

The discovery of the Lost City made news across the nation. The *New York Times* reported, "Buried beneath the drifting sands of southern Nevada has been discovered the 'Lost City of the West,' proof that, antedating the birth of Christ, a now-vanquished race flourished in what today is the state of Nevada. And *Time* magazine breathlessly noted, "In Nevada, an expedition from the Museum of the American Indian [Manhattan], called in by Governor James Graves Scrugham to examine the great cliff city [Pueblo Grande de Nevada], which he had discovered personally, threw up sand all winter over a stretch six miles long, baring adobes ranging from scooped-out hollows in the earth to extensive stone apartment-buildings that sheltered whole clans . . . the artifacts found seemed to date Pueblo Grande before the Aztec culture, which Cortez and other Spaniards found flourishing in Mexico and the Southwest in the 16th century."

In 1926, Scrugham lost his bid for reelection, but Harrington continued to work on the various sites until about 1938. He excavated a number of caves as well as one of the ancient salt mines. In addition to finding baskets, clothing, pottery, weapons, and stone tools, Harrington uncovered more than four dozen buried skeletons, some wrapped in colored shrouds and wearing jewelry. As a result of federal assistance, engineered by Congressman James Scrugham (he was elected to the US House of Representatives in 1932), Harrington gained the help of members of the Civilian

Conservation Corps (CCC) from 1933 to 1938. The workers conducted many of the excavations and, in 1935, built a museum to showcase the artifacts being recovered. The adobe museum building, originally called the Boulder Dam Park Museum, was unique: It was built adjacent to one of the Lost City dig sites. Additionally, Harrington was responsible for designing all of the exhibits, and he personally constructed several of them. In its early years, the museum building also doubled as the offices of the National Park Service's Boulder Dam Park (now known as Lake Mead National Recreation Area).

Harrington accepted the position of curator of the Southwest Museum in Los Angeles in 1928 but he continued working on the Lost City excavations for another decade. He wanted to inventory all the sites in Moapa Valley and excavate as many ruins as was possible. His survey listed seventy-seven ruins on a 16-mile stretch of the Muddy River. At that same time, one of his colleagues, Irwin Hayden, started uncovering a site that became known as Mesa House, a massive pueblo complex built in a courtyard fashion that appeared to contain eighty-four rooms and single-family dwellings. According to Evans, "Harrington believed that these single-story adobe structures were the precursors to the gigantic multistory pueblos that these people built in New Mexico and Arizona, after they left the valley sometime around AD 1100."

Harrington recognized that he was working against the clock, which was part of the reason for his long and continued involvement in the project. The construction of Hoover Dam, completed in 1935, meant that the waters of the Colorado River would soon cover nearly all of the Lost City. Between 1933 and 1935, he oversaw the excavations of seventeen more pueblos. Toward the end, the CCC team members were literally removing artifacts and fragments as water was starting to lap at their feet.

The filling of Lake Mead behind Hoover Dam essentially ended much of the work to uncover the Lost City. Some ruins were restored above the high-water line—including those near the museum—but the serious digging was over. In recent years, the museum has been able to purchase several additional sites not submerged by Lake Mead using various grants, and continues to catalog and preserve them for future generations. The best place to see the thousands of items saved from the flooding of the valley is the Lost City Museum in Overton. Hundreds of artifacts, ranging from obsidian knife blades to ornate baskets and pottery, are displayed in the museum. The original building, now called the Anasazi Wing, contains a significant number of the things uncovered by Harrington and his staff in the 1920s and '30s. In 1981, the Fay Perkins Wing was added, which encloses an archaeological dig site that includes an actual Pueblo foundation excavated by the CCC in 1935. The display reconstructs how the site was prepared as well as how the staff excavated the location and removed artifacts.

On the grounds around the museum are several reconstructions of Pueblo dwellings. For instance, in front of the building is a replica of a traditional Basketmaker pit house (visitors enter through the roof and climb in using a crude wooden ladder) built in the 1930s by CCC members using wood from indigenous trees and locally made adobe. To the rear of the facility is a reconstruction of the Pueblo-style aboveground adobe dwellings. CCC members erected the complex of small, round huts on top of the original foundations. While the structures are somewhat fragile—don't try to climb onto the roofs—you are permitted to crawl into the buildings. Of course, as you sit in semidarkness, smelling the earthy interior of the adobe hut and marveling at how much cooler it is inside the structure than it is outside, you can't help but wonder what happened to the people who could build such things. Where did they go?

CHAPTER 10

The First National Bank of Winnemucca Robbery

At about noon on September 19, 1900, three men, dressed in the clothing of working cowboys, walked into the First National Bank in Winnemucca and demanded gold from the bank's safe. Two of the men pointed pistols at the three bank clerks (Mr. Calhoun, Mr. Hill, and Mr. McBride), as well as W. S. Johnson, a horse buyer who happened to be in the bank at the wrong time. The third one, a man with a scruffy blond beard, grabbed the bank manager, George Nixon, and pressed a large knife to his throat. He suggested that Nixon open the safe as quickly and quietly as possible so that no one would be hurt.

Shaken but calm, Nixon spun the dial on the great safe to the proper set of numbers. With a click, the safe unlocked and the bearded man, still hanging on to Nixon, reached inside and extracted three bags full of gold coins. He tossed them into a larger ore sack that he had brought along, and then led Nixon to the banker's private office, where he had the manager open his

The First National Bank of Winnemucca, site of a robbery that some insist was carried out by Butch Cassidy and his Wild Bunch gang

personal money drawer and empty the contents—$10 and $20 gold coins—into the bag.

The bank robbers ushered the five hostages—Nixon, the three clerks, and Johnson—to a small yard behind the bank. There, while the blond-bearded bandit pointed a gun at the men, the other two climbed over the back fence and ran down an alley to get the horses. The blond desperado slowly backed up to the wooden fence, his gun pointed at the five men still standing with their hands in the air. He warned them not to sound an alarm or he would have to shoot. Then he hopped the fence and disappeared.

As soon as the robbers were out of sight, Nixon pulled a revolver he had hidden in his pocket and ran back into the bank, followed by the others. He rushed into the street in front of the bank building and began firing shots into the air, yelling that the bank had just been robbed. Inside the bank, Johnson snatched a rifle displayed in a decorative wall rack and returned to the backyard. He climbed over the fence and looked around for the thieves and their horses. He spotted them riding away in the alley, aimed carefully at one, and fired, but the gun was not loaded.

Meanwhile, Deputy Sheriff George Rose, who heard Nixon's shots, grabbed his own rifle and bolted from his office in the Humboldt County Courthouse. Wanting to see exactly what was happening, he climbed a nearby windmill, and spotted the three outlaws, who apparently had encountered a problem while trying to race out of town. After leaving the alley, they had turned onto Second Street, fired at Sheriff Charles McDeid, who had stepped from inside a local saloon to see what all the commotion was, and turned a corner so sharply that the heavy ore bag filled with the gold coins had slipped from the horse and fallen into the street. Not wanting to leave without their plunder, the three reined their horses, spun around, and headed back to the bag in the street. As one of the men dismounted and handed the bag to a second one, the third fired several more shots to discourage anyone from pursuing them.

As this was happening, one of the bank employees, Calhoun, had followed the bank robbers on foot. He ran around a corner and encountered the thieves as they were attempting to retrieve the fallen bag of money. According to one newspaper account, Calhoun was fired upon by one of the robbers and dived behind a fence. As he cowered there, another Winnemucca citizen, Christ Lane, who lived in a cottage on the street where the bag fell, heard the shooting and decided to tell the noisemakers to stop shooting their weapons in city limits. He opened a window and started to yell at the men but quickly jumped back when his complaint was answered with a shot fired in his direction.

Having regained their loot, the robbers headed east on the Golconda Road. Deputy Rose, who had witnessed most of the action from the windmill, scampered to the ground and ran to the nearby train spur, where a small switch engine was sitting. He commanded the train crew to steam up and chase the outlaws. In the meantime, the three robbers, who had a considerable head start, rode to the Sloan Ranch, located about eight miles from town. There they changed horses, stealing three fresh equines that, ironically, belonged to George Nixon (including, it has been reported, his favorite one).

Almost like something out of one of the Westerns that would become popular several decades later, the three raced east, with Deputy Rose riding on the front of the little engine gaining on them. When he was close enough to use his rifle, Rose took aim and began scattering shots in the direction of the fleeing thieves. According to David W. Toll, who wrote about the robbery in the May-June 1983 issue of *Nevada Magazine*, Rose managed to wound one of the horses but lost the robbers when they reached a place where a barbed-wire fence had been cut and they could head north, away from the train tracks. Apparently, a few miles ahead, near the Humboldt River, the trio had a small camp with more fresh horses. After transferring their saddles, supplies, and the money to the new horses, they rode off.

Back in Winnemucca, Sheriff McDeid formed several posses and set out to catch the bad men. Despite those efforts and a close call—one posse nearly caught up to the robbers near Clover Valley but couldn't keep up—the three outlaws, who had stolen nearly $33,000, disappeared somewhere near the Idaho-Nevada border.

They were never seen again.

In later years, tantalizing clues about the robbery began to crop up. For instance, Toll reports that a few days before the robbery, nine-year-old Lee Case was playing with a couple of friends when they encountered some cowboys sitting near an empty livery stable in town. The men seemed friendly and chatted with Case and his pals. The next day, the boys again ran into the men, who casually asked questions such as the number of deputies in Winnemucca. The small talk seemed harmless at the time.

Additionally, the same three men were spotted in the days before the robbery about ten miles east of town by ten-year-old Vic Button, who rode to school by way of a trail near the river there. The three had set up a camp adjacent to a well in the area. Button, who was accustomed to seeing itinerant cowboys passing through, didn't pay much attention to the men but he did notice that they had the most striking white horse he had ever seen. He decided to ride over to the camp in order to chat with the trio, hoping to find a way to trade for the magnificent animal. Toll says the men laughed off Button's offer as well as another one he made the following day (the second time he brought one of his father's best horses to trade) and on several subsequent days, when he brought different horses from his father's spread, the CS Ranch, to trade. Despite the rebuffs, the men were friendly and seemed to enjoy Button's company, even asking him what he thought was the best and shortest route to reach southern Idaho.

Toll writes that when the posse almost caught up to the robbers in Clover Valley, one of them stood in his saddle and yelled to the lawmen, "Give the white horse to the kid on the CS Ranch!" (Reportedly, they did.)

Banker Nixon pushed hard to recover his money. He reportedly hired the infamous Tom Horn, a "regulator" from Wyoming, who had earned a reputation as a tough-minded, sharp-shooting bounty hunter and enforcer during the cattlemen–sheepmen wars in that state. He also contacted the Pinkerton National Detective Agency, offering one-fourth of the recovered money and guaranteed payment of $1,000 for each of the thieves—alive or dead.

Proving that the local authorities were not exactly proficient at criminal investigations, the campsite near the river wasn't searched until nearly six weeks after the robbery. There, amazingly, lawmen found the torn-up pieces of three letters, which Nixon taped together, then sent to the Pinkerton agency to be analyzed. One dated September 1, 1900, was addressed to C. E. Rowe of Golconda, Nevada (a small town east of Winnemucca), which said cryptically, "Dear Friend: Yours at hand this evening. We are glad to know you are getting along well. In regards to the sale enclosed letter will explain everything. We have left Baggs, so write us at Encampment, Wyoming. Hoping to hear from you soon I am as ever, your friend Mike."

Another, dated August 24, 1900, was on the letterhead of a Wyoming attorney, D. A. Pristine, and signed by a D. A. Preston. In the letter, the author wrote, "Several influential parties are becoming interested and the chances of a sale are becoming favorable." The third, written by the same hand as the second, had no date or salutation. It simply said: "Send me a map of the country and describe as near as you can the place where you found the black stuff so I can go to it. Tell me how you want it handled. You don't know its value. If I can get hold of it first, I can fix a good many things favorable. Say nothing to anyone about it." It was signed with the initial *P*. Toll notes that Douglas A. Preston was an attorney who represented Butch Cassidy as well as other members of the Wild Bunch in their various legal matters.

Often cited as proof that Butch Cassidy and the Sundance Kid led the raid on the Winnemucca bank is a photograph of the two and three other members of their gang, dressed up in fine suits and derby hats, that allegedly was sent to George Nixon by the gang, along with a taunting note thanking him for the money. Unfortunately, as Toll and many others have pointed out, the story is apocryphal. The photo in question was actually sent by the Pinkerton agency to Nixon five months after the robbery, which wanted him to use it to identify the bank robbers.

The photograph, however, does have a fascinating story unrelated to the Winnemucca job. In December 1900, an undercover Wells Fargo detective discovered the photo on display in the John Swartz Photographic Studio in Fort Worth, Texas. The agent recognized one of the men as Will Carver, a former member of the Black Jack Ketchum gang, which he was pursuing. The others in the photo were also identified as Harvey Logan (aka Kid Curry), Harry Longabaugh (aka Harry Alonzo or the Sundance Kid), Ben Kilpatrick (the Tall Texan), and Robert Leroy Parker (Butch Cassidy). According to Anne Meadows, author of *Digging Up Butch and Sundance*, following several robberies a handful of the members of the Wild Bunch rendezvoused in Fort Worth, Texas, to split up the bounty and celebrate. Carver used the occasion to marry his girlfriend, a former prostitute named Lillie Davis. Feeling quite festive, five of the group decided to dress up as bankers and pose for a local photographer. "This proved to be a colossal blunder," Meadows noted.

After he received the photo, as well as mug shots of Cassidy and other members of the gang, Nixon compared them with his recollections of the three men who robbed his bank. In January 1901, he wrote the Pinkertons, "While I am satisfied that Cassidy was interested in the robbery, he was not one of the men who entered the bank." In later correspondence, Nixon wrote that while he certainly would have no problem paying a reward for the capture of Cassidy, the man in the photograph "is the likeness of a man with a great deal squarer-cut face and massive jaws, in fact somewhat of a bulldog appearance, while the man 'Whiskers' struck me as a fact that, in case it was shaven, would have more of a coyote appearance."

Further adding to the evidence that it would be unlikely that Cassidy had participated in the robbery was the fact that on August 29, 1900—twenty-one days before the Winnemucca robbery—Cassidy robbed a train in Tipton, Wyoming, which is about 600 miles northeast of Winnemucca. According to former Nevada State archivist Guy Louis Rocha, since the bank robbers were known to have camped north of Winnemucca ten days before the robbery, "If Cassidy had committed both crimes, it would have entailed making a 600-mile ride from Tipton to Winnemucca in eleven days." To make the journey, Cassidy would have had to ride nearly fifty-five miles per day, and have fresh horses available all along the route.

Nixon, however, did positively identify another of the men in the photo, Harvey Logan (Kid Curry), as having been in the bank. As for the third robber, Nixon wasn't completely certain but said he was "about confident" that it was Harry Alonzo, the Sundance Kid. Despite the less than certain identifications, the Pinkertons decided it was enough and, in May 1901, posted a $6,000 reward for the arrest of the three men. The agency circulated posters with personal descriptions as well as a statement saying that following a thorough investigation, it had been determined that Butch Cassidy and the Sundance Kid "are suspected of being two of the men engaged in this robbery."

While the Pinkertons sought to put as much heat as possible on Butch Cassidy and the Sundance Kid, the outlaws had already put some distance between themselves and the law. In February 1901, the duo, along with Sundance's companion, Etta (or Ethel) Place, sailed from New York to Buenos Aires, Argentina. Upon arriving, they homesteaded land, acquired cattle and sheep, and tried to make a go (more or less) as legitimate ranchers in the remote Cholila Valley of southern Argentina. Using the names James "Santiago" Ryan (Cassidy) and Mr. and Mrs. Harry "Enrique" Place, they maintained a fairly upstanding facade for a few years.

The Pinkertons, however, were persistent and traced the outlaws to Argentina, where they alerted authorities about the pair's true identities. In February 1905, two English-speaking men robbed a bank in Rio Gallegos (about 700 miles south of the Cholila Valley). Despite not fitting the descriptions of the two men, an arrest order was issued for Butch Cassidy and the Sundance Kid. Tipped off that police were coming to pick them up, the two, along with Place, fled Argentina for Chile.

Between 1906 and 1908, the two outlaws bounced around Chile, Argentina, and Bolivia (Place returned to the United States for good in 1905), occasionally breaking horses and working as payroll guards for a tin mine—and continuing to rob small banks. In November 1908, after hijacking a payroll delivery, the two were apparently killed during a shootout in Bolivia with federal soldiers.

As for the Winnemucca robbery, no one was ever arrested for the crime and the reward was never claimed. According to David Toll, over the years several theories have circulated regarding who was behind the heist. The most accepted version is that members of the Wild Bunch, probably including the Sundance Kid but sans Butch Cassidy, held up the bank and escaped with the money. Toll said that a variation of that theory is that C. E. Rowe or some other local may have tipped off the gang about how easy it would be to rob the bank.

Others, however, insist banker George Nixon and his friend George Wingfield, a prominent local gambler and miner, planned the robbery. According to this legend, Nixon needed the money so he could back Wingfield in investing in the newly discovered mining boomtown of Goldfield. It is true that shortly after the robbery, Wingfield turned up in Goldfield backed by Nixon's financial muscle and began buying lucrative mine properties. Within five years of the robbery, Nixon was a US senator, while Wingfield was considered the richest man in Nevada because of his mining, banking, and property holdings. While it's a tempting conspiracy theory, it's an unlikely one since Nixon was already wealthy enough to back Wingfield without stolen loot from his own bank, and Wingfield was so well known that someone would have recognized him had he been involved in the robbery.

Following the success of the 1969 movie, *Butch Cassidy and the Sundance Kid*, the town of Winnemucca began celebrating Butch Cassidy Days, which included a re-enactment of the shootout at the First National Bank. No one seemed to care that Butch Cassidy never actually committed that particular crime. Perhaps "Kid Curry Days" or "Sundance Kid Days" or "We're-Not-Exactly-Sure-Who-Did-It Days" didn't sound as impressive.

CHAPTER 11

The Unknown Fate of Roy Frisch

On the evening of Friday, March 22, 1934, Mrs. Frisch had invited a few friends over for a game of bridge. Her son, Roy, who lived with her (and his two sisters) in a spacious 3,091-square-foot bungalow at 247 Court Street, decided to get out of the house and catch a film, *Gallant Lady*, at the Majestic Theater, which was located about four blocks northeast. At the time, Roy J. Frisch was forty-one years old and working as the chief cashier at the Riverside Bank in Reno, which was owned by George Wingfield, often described as the wealthiest and most powerful man in the state of Nevada. The bank was actually tucked inside Wingfield's Riverside Hotel.

At about 7:45 p.m., Frisch, who had also served as a member of the Reno City Council, said goodbye to his mother and her friends and walked out the front door. According to Nevada historian Phillip I. Earl, who has researched Frisch, the banker headed two blocks east on Court Street and turned north at the Washoe County Courthouse (on the corner of Court and Virginia streets).

He crossed the Virginia Street Bridge, which spans the Truckee River, and turned east on First Street. From there he walked two more blocks to the theater.

Frisch bought a ticket and entered the theater to watch the 84-minute melodrama. At about 9:30 p.m., after the movie ended, Frisch began the return journey home. This time, he chose to walk back via First Street to Sierra Street, and then followed Sierra to Court. Sometime between 9:45 p.m. and 10:15 p.m., he encountered a friend at the corner of Sierra and Court Streets and exchanged pleasantries for a few minutes. From there, he walked west on Court Street toward his house, which was about two blocks away.

He was never seen again.

The following morning, his mother went to awaken him for work and discovered he had not slept in his bed. Concerned that something might have happened to him, she called the bank and several of his friends—but no one had seen him—before contacting the Reno Police Department. The police interviewed anyone who might have encountered him that night and when nothing came of that, alerted federal authorities, who began a nationwide manhunt. Local papers printed notices asking anyone who might have information about Frisch to step forward and offered a $1,000 reward.

Of course, part of the reason for all the attention to the disappearance of a middle-age, bespectacled banker who lived with his mother was that several months earlier Frisch had testified before a grand jury investigating whether the Riverside Bank was involved in a scam perpetrated by two well-known Reno gamblers/pimps/organized-crime figures named William J. Graham and James C. McKay. In the 1920s and '30s, Graham and McKay were involved

Roy Frisch Mystery Solution Believed Near by U. S. Agents

S. F. News 2-17-37

The baffling disappearance of Roy J. Frisch, missing Reno bank cashier, may be solved soon, Federal officials said today. Mr. Frisch, a Government witness in the case of William J. Graham and James C. McKay, Reno gamblers convicted in New York Saturday of mail fraud and conspiracy, disappeared on the eve of the first trial, four years ago.

Federal officials have renewed attempt to solve his disappearance, according to William Power Maloney, assistant U. S. attorney, who successfully prosecuted Graham and McKay in New York.

The transfer of John Paul Chase, former companion of George (Baby Face) Nelson, one-time public enemy, from Alcatraz to New York for the recent trial, and his resultant questioning there, indicated the Government was insistent on clearing up the case. Chase has since been returned to Alcatraz.

'Knew Too Much'

Chase had declared in Alcatraz that the Reno confidence ring had hired Nelson to kill Mr. Frisch because Mr. Frisch "knew too much." Chase is now serving a life term for the murder of two Federal agents in a gun battle in which Nelson was slain.

Also taken to New York during the trial was Fatso Negri, who was tried in San Francisco with a group of others, charged with harboring Nelson.

Mr. Maloney said Negri had described conversations in which Nelson said, "We killed Frisch," and threatened to "put the finger" on his employers if they did not "come through with more dough."

"Now is a good time to renew the Frisch investigation," said Mr. Maloney. "Maybe a lot of people who were afraid to talk before will loosen up now."

Federal officials said they had "no doubt" that Mr. Frisch had been killed by Nelson. One official indicated Nelson had been employed by Graham at one time. On the witness stand Graham specifically denied knowing Nelson. The sole testimony advanced on Mr. Frisch was by John T. McLaughlin, a G-man, who reported on a fruitless search for Mr. Frisch.

Ambushed in Reno

Chase's confession said he and Nelson had been riding along the street, had seen Mr. Frisch, and that Nelson had leaped from the car, hid behind a bush and then slugged Mr. Frisch with the butt of his gun as he passed.

Chase's story was that Nelson had dragged Frisch into the car, and had taken him to a nearby garage, where Mr. Frisch was transferred to a car owned by William Golder, San Francisco.

Nelson then shot Mr. Frisch through the head, Chase's confession continued, and the body was taken to a depression near an abandoned mine 150 miles southeast of Reno, in the direction of Yerington, and buried in a shallow grave after Mr. Frisch's clothing had been removed and the body burned.

Additional information had been received regarding the case, Asst. U. S. Atty. Miles N. Pike of Reno said.

Frisch Formerly Cashier

"The new information checks in with other things we know, and we are hopeful the case will be solved before very long," Mr. Pike declared.

The News learned that U. S. Atty. E. P. Carville has started for Reno from Washington.

Mr. Frisch had been cashier of the

now defunct Riverside Bank in Reno, where confidence men had sent their victims to convert drafts and securities into cash. He had testified before the Federal Grand Jury which indicted Graham and McKay in 1934.

Sentencing of Graham and McKay was postponed a second time today because Justice Willis Van Devanter is still ill with a slight cold.

ROY FRISCH.
Murdered 'because he knew too much.'

Frisch Case May Be Solved Soon

Jrnl. 3-1-37 / 2-15-37

Additional information has been received recently regarding the disappearance of Roy J. Frisch, missing Reno bank cashier, and government agents are "hopeful the case will be solved soon," federal authorities revealed Tuesday.

Frisch dropped out of sight on March 22, 1934, on the eve of a trip to New York where he was to testify at the first mail fraud trial of James C. McKay and William J. Graham.

McKay and Graham, who were found guilty Saturday at the conclusion of their third trial, are to appear before Judge Van Devanter at 10:30 a.m. Wednesday in New York City for sentencing on four counts which carry a maximum of 17 years in prison and $13,000 fine each.

William Power Maloney, assistant United States attorney who successfully prosecuted the two Reno gamblers, told the Nevada State Journal that the search for Frisch would be renewed immediately.

"Now that we've given Graham and McKay a kick in the pants," Maloney said, "it's a good time to renew the Frisch investigation. Maybe a lot of people who were afraid to talk before will loosen up now."

Asked if Federal Bureau of Investigation agents were in Reno now, Maloney declared that he "couldn't disclose that."

Reno federal officials asserted the search for Frisch had gone on continuously since he disappeared, with one authority adding, "We have received new information recently and are hopeful the case will be solved before very long because it is information that checks with other facts. I am not at liberty, however, to comment on the nature of the new information."

Frisch, cashier of the now-defunct Riverside bank which

ROY J. FRISCH
Missing Since '34

figured prominently in the McKay - Graham trials, testified before the federal grand jury in New York which indicted the pair in 1934.

He returned to Reno and on March 22, 1934—three and a half months before the first trial which ended in a jury disagreement—told members of his family he was going to a show. He has not been seen since.

The mysterious disappearance of banker Roy Frisch in 1934 has been the subject of considerable attention over the years, including these 1937 articles in the *San Francisco News* and the *Nevada State Journal*.

in just about anything illegal (or immoral) in the Biggest Little City. Before and after gambling was legalized in 1935, the two owned the Bank Club, off Douglas Alley in downtown Reno, at the time reportedly the biggest casino in the world. In January 1934, Graham and McKay were indicted on federal charges of mail fraud, stemming from their involvement in a swindle to cheat gullible investors of money allegedly won on out-of-state horse races. The two were quickly whisked off to New York to be put on trial.

According to reports, Graham and McKay's scam usually started out by luring an unsuspecting subject, usually an out-of-town gambler, with a planted purse filled with money. When the Good Samaritan returned the purse, he or she was offered as a reward a tip on a long-shot horse race being held in some distant location, such as Texas. When the horse won, the subject was asked to put up good-faith money to show that he could have covered the loss if the horse had lost. That money was usually deposited in Wingfield's Riverside Bank, where Frisch was the main cashier. The mark was given a ticket and told he could cash out the bet—an amount far more than he had deposited at the bank—at the distant track. But when the mark tried to collect his winnings, there was, of course, no money. Naturally, the good-faith money also had disappeared. Occasionally, the scam was done with a stock-market tip, although the result was always the same.

While many of the victims were too embarrassed to report the crime to the police, a few did contact authorities and lodge formal complaints. A grand jury was summoned to investigate the charges, and Frisch was called to testify. According to Elizabeth Raymond, author of a biography of George Wingfield, Frisch told jurors about dates, amounts of money, and the identities of those who received the money. Interestingly, immediately after he testified, Frisch was assigned a police guard. But on that night in March, days after he had received a subpoena to appear as a witness in Graham and McKay's trial, Frisch was alone and unprotected.

In addition to being close associates of Wingfield, Graham and McKay were also tight with a number of notorious gangsters, some of whom would lay low in Reno or other parts of northern Nevada when things got too hot in other parts of the country. The two were known to have helped Alvin Karpis and members of the Ma Barker gang hide out in northern Nevada and Reno for a time in 1933. In March 1934, gangland figures Baby Face Nelson (Lester M. Gillis) and John Paul Chase were hanging out in Reno before a planned rendezvous with the John Dillinger gang.

Nelson was a known associate of Graham and McKay and worked occasionally as a chauffeur for the two.

Not surprisingly, police immediately suspected Nelson of being involved in Frisch's disappearance. Writer David W. Toll, who explored the crime in an online article, said after Chase had been arrested and sent to Alcatraz for several other crimes later that year, the gangster told investigators that he and Nelson had indeed followed Frisch from the theater. "Nelson had blocked Frisch's path with the black Buick sedan he was driving, and then picked a fight with him. He knocked Roy down, and then threw him into the back of the car. They had driven out of town, he said, eventually pulling off the highway near Yerington, where they killed Frisch," Toll wrote.

In its July 14, 1935, edition, the *Chicago Daily Tribune* reported that the "solution of the mysterious disappearance nearly

16 months ago of Roy J. Frisch, Reno banker, appeared nearer tonight as authorities investigated the story Frisch was slain by the late gangster, [Baby Face] Nelson." According to the *Tribune*, J. Edgar Hoover, head of the FBI, confirmed that Chase "admitted he witnessed Frisch's slaying" and federal, state, city, and county authorities were renewing the investigation, which had previously been stalled. The article said that authorities were considering bringing Chase to Reno to help locate Frisch's remains.

"Frisch's body was reported to have been disposed of in a shallow grave near a mine shaft several miles from Reno after Nelson had burned his clothes and destroyed other means of identification," the *Tribune* said. "According to Chase's story, Nelson hit Frisch on the head with a revolver and threw him in an automobile. Several miles from Reno, Chase said, Nelson shot the banker. Rewards were offered [in the aftermath of Frisch's disappearance]. Posses searched the Truckee River and Lake Tahoe regions. Other recruits and officers were sent into the depths of abandoned mine shafts."

Chase agreed to lead authorities to the place where he said that he and Nelson had buried Frisch's body, but when he was released into the custody of federal agents he couldn't locate the site. The FBI concluded that Chase was lying and had only wanted a break from prison life. The only other witness to the alleged abduction and murder was Baby Face Nelson. Unfortunately, Nelson, who went on a killing spree shortly after leaving Reno in April 1934, was gunned down during a shoot-out with FBI agents near Barrington, Illinois, in November 1934.

Another theory that has gained credence over the years is that Nelson and Chase murdered Frisch and drove his body to one of Wingfield's mining properties in Central Nevada, where they dumped the body at the bottom of a deep shaft. Toll has written about a mysterious encounter he had in the 1960s with a man who claimed he knew what had happened to Frisch. In 1934, the man and a partner had leased the Fairview Mine from George Wingfield. They had been installing a new pump in the main shaft when a strange, black car drove up to the mine. Neither the man nor his partner was in the mine that day, but his partner's wife saw a car containing three men drive to the main mine shaft and, a short time later, it departed with only two people inside the vehicle.

"After a few weeks, the pump started to act up," the man told Toll. "The filter kept clogging up with some kind of gummy fibrous material. It would start all right, and run fine for a while, but then the filter would clog again and it would heat up, and I'd have to take it apart and clean off this stuff I'd never seen in a mine before."

Over time, the problem finally lessened but the man decided to set some of the gunk aside to have it analyzed. A short time later, he took his sample to a doctor in nearby Fallon, who was able to identify it as human hair from a white, middle-age male. "He never told anyone but me, he said. At the time, weeks after the disappearance, his partner and his wife convinced him they didn't want to get involved in anything involving George Wingfield and Baby Face Nelson," Toll wrote. A postscript to the story is that Toll never wrote down the man's name or other details because he figured it would be impossible to find any proof about the story's authenticity more than three decades after Frisch had disappeared. But, he wrote, it's a story he continues to believe is true.

When the Graham-McKay trial finally began in April 1934, the Riverside Bank was described as "a place where no questions were asked," and Frisch, no longer able to defend himself, was said to have looked the other way regarding the "mystery transactions." Bank owner George Wingfield appeared as perplexed as anyone regarding Frisch's whereabouts, musing that perhaps his former employee had decided to "fade out." The trial ended in a hung jury, and a second trial a year later had the same result. In February 1938, the government tried once more and was able to convict the two "confidence men," as well as two associates, of swindling victims out of nearly $2.5 million.

William Power Maloney, an assistant US attorney involved with the case, told the *New York Times* on February 13, 1938, that the verdict marked "emancipation day for the whole state of Nevada." The *Times* story also noted that John Paul Chase was scheduled to testify at the 1934 trial that he and Nelson had killed Frisch, but just before his eagerly anticipated appearance, he recanted his confession. In 1939, Graham and McKay were fined $11,000 each and sentenced to nine years in the federal penitentiary for mail fraud. About a week after the verdict, the *Times* noted in another story about the case that "hope is expressed, though without a great deal of confidence, it is true, that someone who knows now may tell the inside of the Frisch disappearance." But no one ever came forward.

In 1941, Frisch was formally declared dead—although it's said his mother kept the porch light on for many years after his disappearance in the hope that he might see it and return. While the FBI and Reno police closed their Frisch files, others continued to hypothesize about what really happened to the banker. In the 1990s, a new theory surfaced: Nelson and Chase murdered Frisch and buried his body in the spacious backyard of Wingfield's splendid Classical Revival mansion at 219 Court Street. This version of events was dripping in irony since Wingfield's home was only two houses east of the Frisch house. The owner of the former Wingfield property gave authorities permission to search the backyard, but nothing was ever found. Interestingly, Wingfield's historic home, built in 1907, was itself destroyed in 2001 by an arsonist, who has never been caught. In 2006, the city approved a 499-unit condominium project for the site but to date nothing has been built.

In the book, *Washoe County, NV Sheriff's Office*, produced in 2004 by the Washoe County Sheriff's Office, the authors note, "Witnesses were identified that would indicate several different scenarios for disposing of the remains of Roy Frisch. Everything from taking the body out onto Lake Tahoe and then weighting it and tossing it into the cold dark depths of the lake to thoughts that it had been buried in the backyard of the Wingfield Estate on Court Street had been pondered."

In the end, perhaps the only thing for sure is that no one will ever know what really happened to Roy Frisch.

CHAPTER 12

Area 51: The Truth Is Out There

There are no streetlights in the tiny eastern Nevada hamlet of Rachel. There are few porch lights or neon signs. At night, when it grows dark, only the stars, the moon, and the headlights of the occasional automobile illuminate the high desert landscape. This is a part of rural Nevada where there is very little light pollution. The night skies are inky black, clear, and filled with thousands of tiny pinholes of stellar energy. The darkness offers the protection of being unseen as well as the fear of what can't be seen. Night is when the imagination can take hold, weaving tales of the lost, forbidden, secretive, or unfamiliar.

With that in mind, it shouldn't be surprising that remote Rachel—located about 115 miles northeast of Las Vegas—is the gateway to America's last, great unknown place: Area 51, also called Dreamland, Groom Lake (its geographic designation), or Paradise Ranch (its original, rather tongue-in-cheek name). The stories of what allegedly goes on at Area 51, a secluded hunk of land southwest of Rachel, are legend. What is known is that Area 51 is home

COURTESY OF THE NEVADA COMMISSION ON TOURISM

Who knows what secrets lurk inside of Area 51, located deep in the Nevada desert?

to a secret US military base tucked inside 4,742 square miles of restricted land and air that is part of the Nevada Test Site, where America has tested its nuclear weapons arsenal since 1951.

Since the base was established (on the site of an old World War II airstrip) in the mid-1950s, there have been bizarre rumors about it housing strange aircraft, UFOs, and captured aliens, among other amazing stories. Aerial photos, which you can check out online at various sites, show a complex of several dozen small rectangular buildings, a hangar, offices, several runways, and other structures. One popular story is that these structures are only the tip of the iceberg—and beneath the site is a massive, hidden compound that stretches some forty levels underground and includes subterranean rail systems that link it to the military facilities at Los Alamos and White Sands in New Mexico as well as to Los Angeles.

Of course, construction of that scale would be difficult to hide, no matter how remote the site, because of the sheer number of construction workers that would be needed for such a project.

What's known about the base, originally referred to as Paradise Ranch, or the Ranch, is that it was apparently constructed, under the auspices of the CIA, to test the U-2 spy plane. The supersecret plane, designed to fly over enemy territory (namely, the USSR during the Cold War) at extremely high altitudes, was built at a secret facility in Burbank, California, then flown in pieces to the Ranch, where it was assembled and tested. In his book, *Dreamland*, Phil Patton wrote that, in 1960, following the successful development of the U-2, the Ranch became the site for developing and testing the next spy plane, the AR-12 (later known as the SR-71 or Blackbird), which could fly even higher and faster than its predecessor.

It's also around this time that the name Area 51 began to be associated with the base. There are several versions of the story of how the name was derived, although the most likely seems to be that "Area 51" was its location on the grid map of the Nevada Test Site that was created in the 1950s by the Atomic Energy Commission. Starting in about 1967, Area 51 was used to test the limits of captured enemy aircraft. Under the auspices of the Air Force and the CIA, American pilots flew various Soviet aircraft (mostly MiG fighters) over Area 51 during war games and training exercises.

In the mid-1970s, the US government began experimenting with "stealth" technology aircraft, which were planes that could not be detected by conventional radar because of their unique shape and building materials, including reflective surfaces that deflected electromagnetic waves. The first models, which were tested at Area

51, included an airplane code-named Have Blue, an early, smaller, less stable version of what eventually became the F-117 Stealth Fighter, and Tacit Blue, a bizarre, rectangular stealth technology reconnaissance vehicle. Only two of the Have Blue planes were built and both crashed, while the Tacit Blue prototype was retired and, in 1996, put on display in the National Museum of the United States Air Force at Wright-Patterson Air Force Base in Ohio.

Starting in the early 1980s, Area 51 became the secret testing ground for the F-117 Nighthawk stealth fighter plane. The base was used for night test flights, F-117 weapons testing, and for training the first generation of pilots who would fly the planes. The F-117 squadron was later transferred to the Tonopah Test Range (another restricted base, located 30 miles southeast of the old mining town of Tonopah) and, in 1989, to Holloman Air Force Base in New Mexico. It was around the time of the latter transfer that the existence of the F-117 was revealed to the general public.

Following the relocation of the F-117 program, Area 51 was used to test other experimental aircraft including the Bird of Prey, a futuristic, spear-shaped stealth plane that was never put into mass production (the only model ever made is also displayed at Wright-Patterson). It also has been used to test various models of stealth missiles. There have been rumors of other aircraft tested at Area 51, including the Aurora, a replacement for the SR-71 spy plane using stealth technology, and the TR3A Black Manta, allegedly a successor to the F-117, although there is no evidence that either plane has ever existed.

Some insist that the testing of various secret aircraft over Area 51 throughout the years is the real source of the stories about alien spaceships. They say that these often unusual looking, experimental planes—some of which the public may not even be aware exist—were what observers wanted to believe contained strange visitors from other worlds.

One mythical craft in particular, a so-called stealth blimp, has long been the source of intrigue. In the televised program, *Unsolved History: Area 51*, the producers speculated that periodic reports of mysterious V-shaped, lighted objects in the sky may have been sightings of a secret, experimental triangular-shaped dirigible made with stealth technology. The show hypothesized that the craft, said to be completely quiet and with a series of either white or amber lights in a V or triangle pattern on the underside, could be the reason for unexplained UFO sightings in the late 1990s and early 2000s in places like Phoenix and southern Illinois. Additionally, the January 2009 issue of *Popular Science* revealed that the US government is developing the next generation of stealth bomber, a bat wing–shaped airplane that will replace the B-2 stealth bomber by 2018. Could prototypes of this plane already have been tested at Area 51?

However, many UFO enthusiasts claim that after an alien spacecraft crashed in Roswell, New Mexico, in 1947, the wreckage and remains of the aliens were taken to Area 51 for study. Phil Patton wrote of a man, Bob Lazar, who said he worked in the 1980s on a flying saucer at Area 51 that was based on alien technology. Lazar said the ship was powered by "element 115," a reddish orange substance that fueled antimatter reactors that could bend gravity. He also claimed to have seen one of the aliens assisting Area 51 scientists.

Many of those who seek to believe the legends about Area 51 and aliens have developed their own totems for possibly catching a glimpse of something that might vindicate their beliefs. For example, for many years some UFO aficionados were obsessed with the so-called Black Mailbox, an overly large, round-topped mailbox that is actually white (it was originally black). The box, located a few miles east of Rachel, is a real mail container owned by a local rancher, Steve Medlin. In the 1990s, Lazar and others used it as an easy-to-find marker for those hoping to catch a glimpse of the wondrous crafts he said he spotted over Area 51; he reported watching a bright disc-shaped light in the sky one night in 1989. Over time, however, the box became an icon or, according to Phil Patton, "the perfect symbol of Dreamland. Of the whole black world, the black budget! It suggested blackmail and *Men in Black* and black helicopters." As the years passed, the box gained its own mythology—believers once shoved letters and messages to the aliens into the box. In 2014, Medlin, tired of people breaking into his mailbox (which he had been forced to padlock), had it removed.

Until the mid-1990s, the believers also could gather at Whitesides Peak and Freedom Ridge, both prime lookout points for Groom Lake and Area 51. Located only a dozen or so miles north of the base, both sites offered unobstructed views of its buildings, hangars, runways, and so forth. Believers would often spend the night at either site hoping to see strange aircraft. Naturally, once they became tourist attractions and began attracting too much attention, including TV crews, the military had them closed to the public in April 1995.

While there is no fence around the perimeter of Area 51, the boundaries are marked with orange poles and warning signs stating that no trespassing is allowed (as well as no photographing). In small print is the sobering threat that security is authorized to use deadly force on anyone who insists on trespassing. There are also said to be motion detectors planted around the perimeter. Several sources report that apparently nonmilitary personnel or military contractors patrol the perimeter. Known as the "camo dudes," these mysterious security forces drive around in unmarked four-wheel-drive vehicles and often wear desert camouflage outfits. They're backed by helicopters, which seemingly appear from nowhere and hover over anyone found near the perimeter. Most of the time, the dudes avoid contact with intruders, preferring to call any violations in to the local sheriff, who drives out to handle them.

Despite the high security, Area 51 legends continue to have a powerful allure. In 1996, the state of Nevada officially designated Nevada State Highway 375, the road through Rachel that skirts around the northern edge of Area 51, the Extraterrestrial Highway. Road signs with flying saucers were erected along the 98-mile stretch between Warm Springs and Crystal Springs. The tongue-in-cheek promotional effort tied in to the release of *Independence Day*, a blockbuster science-fiction film starring Will Smith, Bill Paxton, and Jeff Goldblum that was released in July of that year. The movie, which made more than $800 million worldwide, told the story of a worldwide alien invasion and focused on a group of survivors—who converge at Area 51—that successfully defeats the extraterrestrials. A concrete time capsule marked ID4 (for Independence Day), which contains items and memorabilia donated by the cast and crew of the film (to be opened in 2050), remains planted in front of the Little A'Le'Inn restaurant in Rachel.

Additionally, the town of Rachel, which was only founded in 1973—largely to provide services for workers at the local tungsten mine (now closed)—continues to peddle itself as the UFO Capital of the World. The Little A'Le'Inn is the only business in town and owner Pat Travis sells plenty of alien T-shirts, coffee mugs, greeting cards, posters, and other spacey souvenirs. The diner is well known for its Alien Burger, which you can order "with secretions" (cheese). Out in front of the cafe is a red-and-white sign high on a telephone pole that depicts a flying saucer and contains the words: SELF PARKING.

No word if there have ever been any takers.

CHAPTER 13

Why Did Gangster
Bugsy Siegel Die?

B enjamin Siegel was convinced things were finally looking up. The famous gangster, disparagingly called Bugsy in the popular press because of rumors about his out-of-control, "buggy" behavior, saw that business was starting to improve at the Flamingo Hotel, the elegant resort in Las Vegas on which he had staked his reputation, finances, and future.

At the time, Siegel needed some good news. The Flamingo had taken longer to build than originally planned and cost far more than the original $1 million estimate—about six times more, much of it borrowed from Siegel's organized-crime pals. Siegel had become involved in the project in February 1946 after the original owner, Los Angeles restaurateur Billy Wilkerson, a gambling addict, had run out of money to finish the hotel. Wilkerson started work on the Flamingo in November 1945 but soon discovered that building materials were scarce in the post-war era, and suppliers wanted exorbitant prices when they were available. The desperate

The luxurious Flamingo Hotel in Las Vegas, pictured here in about 1946, was gangster Benjamin "Bugsy" Siegel's downfall and legacy.

Wilkerson agreed to partner with a group of investors that included Moe Sedway and Gus Greenbaum, associates of gang leader Meyer Lansky. Siegel, a childhood friend of Lansky's, was designated to manage the project and protect the mob's investment.

Over time, Siegel began to exert more control over the project, eventually squeezing out Wilkerson. He managed to intimidate Wilkerson into walking away from the hotel, without ever paying him a dime, and assumed control over every aspect of its construction. In *The Man Who Invented Las Vegas*, a biography of Wilkerson and his often overlooked role in building the Flamingo, author W. R. Wilkerson III (Billy Wilkerson's son) wrote that Siegel "knew little about building a large resort." He said that as the gangster become more demanding and autocratic—insisting on extravagant luxuries and constantly changing the plans—the project costs skyrocketed. Additionally, contractors were ripping off Siegel by delivering building supplies during the day, stealing them back at night, then bringing them back the next day, and charging Siegel for them once again.

Siegel, however, believed in the Flamingo, which he saw as opening a grand era of elegant and classy Miami-style resorts in the southern Nevada desert. He saw this as his big chance to go legitimate. In his eagerness to get the place up and running, Siegel announced he was moving up the grand opening to December 26, 1946, from the original date of March 1, 1947. Perhaps foreshadowing the future, it rained on opening day—who would have predicted a monsoon in the middle of the desert? The customers and celebrities Siegel thought would stream into Las Vegas from Los Angeles to experience his new attraction didn't materialize despite top-notch entertainers like Xavier Cugat and his orchestra, comedian Rose Marie, and singer Jimmy Durante. The hotel rooms also weren't finished, so guests had to head to the rival El Rancho Vegas and Last Frontier to book accommodations. Whether due to cheating dealers or bad luck, the Flamingo's table games leaked money: The casino reportedly lost $300,000 in the first two weeks. In fact, things were so bad that Siegel was forced to shut down the joint two weeks later.

However, the reopening on March 1, 1947, when the rooms were ready, went well. The Andrews Sisters performed to packed crowds in the showroom, and soon the casino was making a profit. Siegel continued to be cautious, though; some might even say paranoid. He hunkered down in a bunker-like suite that had hidden escape routes, had the room locks changed weekly, and kept a car at the ready in the garage for a quick getaway. He regularly shuttled between Las Vegas, Los Angeles (where both his wife and his mistress lived), and Miami, the latter to reassure Lansky that the money that had been invested would soon be paid back. Still, he had to suspect that his partners' patience was wearing thin. According to W. R. Wilkerson III, despite all of Siegel's efforts, "It was too little, too late . . . the image of the man they had trusted to mastermind their most important project had radically altered."

On the evening of June 20, 1947, in Los Angeles Siegel invited two friends, L.A. gangster Mickey Cohen and actor George Raft, to a relaxing dinner, but they were busy. So Siegel rounded up Alan Smiley, an old gangster pal, along with Jeri Mason, his personal secretary, and Charles Hill, brother of his on-again, off-again girlfriend, Virginia Hill. (Contrary to the Bugsy legend, the hotel was not named by the gangster after the auburn-haired Hill, but rather was named by Wilkerson after he had seen the lanky pink birds in Florida and thought their beauty and elegance would make a good symbol for the hotel.)

The four drove to a restaurant in Ocean Park, a few miles from Virginia Hill's rented mansion in Beverly Hills, where Siegel was staying. (Hill had fought with Siegel and jetted off to Paris in a huff.) After dinner, the group returned to Hill's home, at 810 North Linden Drive. It was about 10:30 p.m. when Siegel and Smiley retired to the living room to talk and smoke.

The two men sat next to each other on a comfortable chintz sofa. The matching floral drapes behind the sofa were about halfway open in front of a row of four, tall, arched French windows. Smiley took a cigarette from the long, narrow wooden box that sat on the Queen Anne–style coffee table and tapped the end twice on the marble top. He lit the cigarette, leaned back, and inhaled deeply. As he blew a stream of smoke through his nose, he noticed the small bronze statue of a nude woman with her arms outstretched that stood on the table. He thought it looked slightly comical.

Siegel picked up a copy of the *Los Angeles Times* and began leafing through the pages. He probably didn't feel the first bullet, which ripped through the back of his head and into his brain. A second blew his eye out of the socket—police later found it about 15 feet from the body. In rapid succession, two other shots whizzed by Smiley, who threw himself on the floor. Two more bullets burrowed into the dying Siegel's chest, finishing the job. The shooter squeezed off three more shots, all of which missed both Siegel and Smiley, before he fled the scene.

Two days later, in a story headlined "Siegel, Gangster Is Slain on Coast," the *New York Times* reported, "The killer, screened by shrubbery, crept up the driveway of the adjoining house and fired an Army-style carbine through a trellis only a few yards from where Siegel sat. At least six bullets ripped into the living room, several narrowly missing Smiley. Neighbors heard the shots and reported that a car roared down the street a few seconds later. Police have no clue."

Other reports indicated that the murder weapon was a 30-caliber US Army carbine and that nine spent shells as well as several cigarette butts were later found outside the living-room windows.

Of course, when it came to determining who might have wanted Siegel dead, there was no shortage of suspects or motives. Over the years, the gangster had made many enemies. Born to poor Russian immigrants in Brooklyn, New York, on February 28, 1906, Siegel saw his father work long and hard for little return—and vowed not to end up that way. At a young age, he began a protection racket, threatening to beat up local pushcart vendors who didn't pay him for his protection. While in his teens, he became close friends with another kid from the neighborhood, Meyer Lansky, and formed the Bug & Meyer Gang, which was involved in bootlegging, illegal gambling, and stealing cars.

By his early twenties, Siegel became an effective contract killer and earned a reputation as a violent hothead who sometimes thought first with his fists and a gun. Lansky has been quoted as saying, "When we were in a fight, Benny would never hesitate. He was even quicker to take action than those hot-blooded Sicilians, the first to start punching and shooting. Nobody reacted faster than Benny." In the late 1930s, Siegel's associates sent him to Los Angeles to set up new protection rackets (primarily extortion from Hollywood unions, studios, and movie stars) and, ultimately, to head the Flamingo project.

In *Playboy's Illustrated History of Organized Crime*, author Richard Hammer speculated that Siegel was ripping off those same mob associates. Hammer believed that Siegel was skimming money from the building fund and giving it to Virginia Hill, who deposited it into a numbered account in Switzerland (in 1966, Hill died mysteriously near Salzburg, Austria; police ruled it a suicide). He wrote that even Siegel's old pal Lansky had allegedly stopped trying to protect him. Lansky later denied playing any part in Siegel's assassination, telling an Israeli newspaper in 1975, "If it was in my power to see Benny alive, he would live as old as [Methuselah]."

Other accounts, however, claim there was a secret meeting of syndicate members in Havana, Cuba, in 1947 that included Lansky as well as gang bosses Frank Costello, Vito Genovese, Joey Adonis, and Charles "Lucky" Luciano, exiled head of the New York organized-crime family and a big investor in the Flamingo. During the meeting, the group, including Lansky, agreed that Siegel needed to be eliminated because he was cheating his partners by skimming and had made such a mess of the Flamingo project.

Writing on the website "The Crime Library," Mark Gribben said the assembled mobsters unanimously agreed to give the contract for taking out Siegel to Charlie Fischetti, a former bodyguard of Al Capone, who had the nickname Trigger Happy. Following the meeting, Siegel flew to Havana to meet with Luciano to ask for more time but was rebuffed by the crime boss, who demanded immediate payment. It's been reported that Siegel refused and angrily stormed out of the meeting, which apparently sealed his fate.

Yet another theory is that Siegel was killed because he had such a high profile in the media that he had become an embarrassment to his more discreet mob partners. Siegel was not averse to publicity, particularly the fawning Hollywood press. During his time in Los Angeles, he was a regular on the society pages, attending many celebrity parties and cultivating friendships with film stars like his childhood friend, actor George Raft, as well as other famous movie people such as Cary Grant, Barbara Hutton, and Jean Harlow. In fact, Raft once said that his handsome friend "was a frustrated actor and secretly wanted a movie career, but he never quite had nerve enough to ask for a part in one of my pictures."

W. R. Wilkerson III offered two other theories for Siegel's assassination: The gangster was either killed by a rival mob boss who coveted his profitable southern California bookmaking operations or murdered by someone hired by the other Las Vegas casino owners who didn't want the New York syndicate moving onto their turf.

Perhaps the most tragic backstory involving Siegel's murder appeared in Warren Robert Hull's book, *Family Secret*, in which he claimed Siegel was shot by Robert McDonald, a WWII war hero (three Purple Hearts, a Silver Star, and a Bronze Star) and son of one of Howard Hughes's personal assistants. According to Hull, McDonald, twenty-seven, was an alcoholic, a regular drug user, and a gambler. He ran up some $25,000 in casino debts to Los Angeles mobster Jack Dragna. Coincidentally, Dragna had just been notified by Luciano to take out Siegel. Knowing that McDonald had been an army sharpshooter, Dragna allegedly told him that he could either do a hit on someone for the mob to eliminate his debt or be killed.

Taken to a home in Beverly Hills—apparently he had no idea who he was to shoot—McDonald hid in the shrubs until he spotted his target and then fired off nine shots before fleeing in a waiting car. Of course, he later read the lurid coverage of the crime in the papers and became aware of who he had killed. The murder seemed to eat at McDonald, who began seeing a psychiatrist. Hull writes that part of his treatment was to confess his part in the Siegel shooting to his wife, Betty Ann, and his parents. The source of Hull's information for the book, in fact, was the senior McDonald, who talked to the writer shortly before his death.

In September 1947, about three months after the Siegel hit, McDonald took his 30-caliber carbine and killed his wife, who apparently had threatened to divorce him during an argument. Horrified at what he had done, he then put the rifle in his mouth and committed suicide (in front of the couple's six-year-old son).

Regardless of who was responsible—police have never solved the murder—actions immediately following Siegel's death would seem to indicate the New York syndicate was involved in his demise. Mere minutes after Siegel was dead, his mob associates, Moe Sedway, Gus Greenbaum, and Morris Rosen, walked into the Flamingo and announced they would now be in charge of the operations. Sedway and Greenbaum had become acquainted with Wilkerson through his heavy gambling. In the mid-1940s, the two managed the El Cortez Hotel in downtown Las Vegas on behalf of the syndicate, a place where Wilkerson dropped plenty of money. When Wilkerson decided to build the Flamingo, he approached them to operate the casino because of their experience in the gambling business. The two agreed to be silent partners and to run the casino for a percent of the gambling profits.

While he no doubt knew that both men were "connected," Wilkerson may not have known the extent of their involvement with the mob. According to W. R. Wilkerson III, Greenbaum was a former bookmaker who was one of the best casino managers in the business (not only did he eventually transform the Flamingo into a profitable enterprise but later he made the Riviera Hotel successful as well). Sedway was one of Lansky's most loyal underlings.

Greenbaum and Sedway immediately purchased the Flamingo from Siegel's Nevada Projects Corporation for $3.9 million and took formal control. In 1948, under Greenbaum's watchful eye, the resort made a profit of $4 million—some believe it was probably much higher and that the rest was skimmed by the mob. Over the next few years, the Flamingo thrived as one of Las Vegas's hottest spots, hosting some of the biggest names in entertainment. In 1955, Greenbaum retired to Arizona but was called back to Las Vegas to manage the new Riviera Hotel (also owned by the syndicate). Three years later, he was eased out of his position at the hotel because of drug and gambling addictions that had become an embarrassment. It has also been rumored that he had started to skim from his own hotel to support his habits. Additionally, his old syndicate pals were concerned that he might talk to authorities should they try to sweat him by tossing him in jail and denying him his drugs. On December 3, 1958, an unknown assailant cut the throats of Greenbaum and his wife while they were in their Phoenix home. No one was ever arrested for the double homicide. Meanwhile, Sedway died in 1952 of a heart attack.

Siegel's original three-story Flamingo Hotel was eventually engulfed by newer, much larger hotel towers. In 1993, Hilton Hotels, which owned the property, demolished the last remnant of the forty-six-year-old resort, the Oregon Building, which had housed Siegel's fortified suite and bulletproof office. While it was an ignominious end to the gangster's grand vision, it was somehow appropriate.

CHAPTER 14

Walker Lake's Sea Serpents

The Paiute people have long told a legend about two sea serpents that lived in Walker Lake. According to the story, the creatures were once human beings, a male and a female, who for some reason were turned into the big, snakelike monsters. Children were cautioned not to make fun of the beasts or to talk in a lighthearted way about them. One day, before the arrival of the white men, a man traveling over the Wassuk Range from East Walker River spotted one of the giant serpents basking on the banks of the lake, below some cliffs. Frightened by the fierce-looking thing, he notched an arrow and fired at it, then let fly another and another. Each time, the arrows merely bounced off its armor-like scales. The man decided to light his arrows on fire. This time, the flaming projectiles pierced the monster's hide and killed it. A year later he returned to find only "big ribs like a cow's or bigger," reported Edward Johnson in his book *History of the Walker River Paiutes*.

Since then, there have been other sightings of some type of huge serpentine creature in the lake, located about 75 miles southeast of Reno. Walker Lake is one of those starkly barren yet beautiful high desert lakes found in Nevada. Perhaps because there is so little vegetation growing around the lake, there is a severe, almost harsh quality to the landscape that is lessened only by the presence of so much water.

Geologically, the lake sits in a long, narrow, natural depression or trough called the Walker Lane, which stretches from Oregon to Death Valley. Scientists believe the lake is a remnant of a prehistoric inland sea known as Lake Lahontan, which covered nearly all of northwestern Nevada during the last ice age (which ended about 10,000 to 15,000 years ago). The lake covers about 50 square miles. It is 18 miles long, about 7 miles wide, approximately 90 feet deep, and has no natural outlet, so its waters dissipate either through absorption in the soil or evaporation. Its primary source is Walker River, which flows in from the north.

The first modern report of any monster sightings in the area appeared in 1868. In a letter to the *Esmeralda Union* newspaper in the mining town of Aurora, Nevada (located about 30 miles west of the lake), a man named Reuben Strathers said he and a friend killed a monster on Brawley Peaks, which is located southwest of Aurora. In the letter, Strathers described a creature with "a head in shape not unlike that of the crocodile, with forefeet near the neck, with tail of enormous length, which lay perfectly quiet, and only the body part moving, which apparently was covered with scales, glistening in the morning sun."

Strathers said that after they had killed the monster, he and his friend drew closer but were soon overpowered by a "sickly" stench. He estimated that the thing was 56 feet long and speculated

A native Paiute fishes on the shores of Walker Lake in this 1924 photo by famed photographer Edward S. Curtis.

that it was most likely a previously unknown type of reptile that probably came from Mono Lake, which is 5 miles south of where the creature was found. He said that it probably was the source of some of the Indian superstitions regarding Mono Lake. Unfortunately, Strathers never produced any proof of his unusual kill and the story was soon forgotten.

The next report about Walker Lake's sea serpents cropped up in August 1883 in the *Walker Lake Bulletin*, a newspaper published in Hawthorne, Nevada, located a few miles south of the lake. An article noted that the Paiutes had long told stories about the existence of the monsters, and now there was proof. The paper said that local Paiutes camped on the shore "were awakened by a horrible soul-shrinking screech. Looking out, they plainly discerned two monster serpents fighting."

According to the piece, "The battle continued for some time and finally extended to dry land, where one of the ghoul reptiles was seriously wounded." The Paiutes killed the severely wounded creature and gave it to a white man, said the paper. After it was dead, the monster was stretched out and measured. Allegedly, it was "exactly seventy-nine feet seven inches and a quarter in length." The paper, however, published no additional reports about this particular serpent or the disposition of the body.

In 1907, the *Washington Herald* (Washington, Indiana) recounted the story of a Goldfield, Nevada, miner who said he had seen a "monster sea serpent" in Walker Lake. Don Cornelison, "a mining man of good reputation for veracity," said he and a friend, John McCorry, spotted the swimming reptile while fishing in a boat about half a mile from the lake's northern shore. "Cornelison says that at first sight he took the serpent for a man in a skiff, and when it disappeared for a moment he thought the boat had capsized, and rowed toward the spot, when it suddenly reappeared, giving them a good view of its proportions, which they estimated to be about thirty feet in length and six feet across the back," the paper said. The article quoted another man, Peters, who also claimed to have seen one of the serpents "reposing in shallow water." When he tried to get a closer look, the creature quickly swam off into deeper waters.

That same year, however, the *Lyon County Times* in Yerington, located about forty-five miles northwest of the lake, noted it had been about a quarter century since the last report of any large snake creatures in Walker Lake and suggested the stories were nothing more than Indian superstition. It admitted there had been periodic sightings by white men, although the size and shape of the monsters they had seen were different from the one glimpsed by the Native Americans. "It is more than likely that what they have seen is [a] long line of swan or other water fowl, which abound on the lake, swimming on its surface," the paper said.

Despite its skepticism, the *Lyon County Times* also noted later that year that the president of Stanford University, Professor David Star Jordan, an expert on prehistoric fish, including ichthyosaurs, was interested in Walker Lake's serpents and planned to "capture the snake and after a thorough dissection, will send its remains to the Smithsonian Institute." Again, the story seemed to reach a dead end as there were no other accounts of Jordan or anyone else fishing for sea serpents in Walker Lake.

Two years later, the *Reno Evening Gazette* printed an article with the headline "Walker Lake Sea Serpent No Joke," claiming that several people had seen a white man wrestling some kind of snake creature in the lake. The paper noted that the story turned out to be a hoax, but it quoted a detective who had studied the lake and found that none of the local Indians would ever go into the lake for fear of the monsters. The *Reno Evening Gazette* also told of a Japanese railroad worker who tried to swim ashore from a boat but disappeared into the lake. The paper added, "It was believed that the monster ate the remains."

Perhaps the strangest allegation surfaced in a *Walker River Bulletin* story in August 1915. The story said that a month earlier there had been some type of violent turbulence on the west side of the lake near Dutch Creek. Some believed the activity was caused by a volcanic eruption in the area while others believed it was created by the sea serpents. According to the *Bulletin*, "After the outburst or upheaval of water, which sent white horses [waves] in every direction, white smoke or fog arose to the crest of Mountain Grant."

Throughout the 1920s and '30s, particularly after a road was constructed around the west edge of the lake, there were semi-regular reports about sightings of some kind of giant snake or fish creature in the lake. In 1934, the *Mineral County Independent* went so far as to print a lengthy feature—with doctored pictures—providing a history of the monster and noting, "There are underground springs feeding into the lake and it is a common belief that there is an underground outlet." Indeed, there have long been stories of an underground passage between Walker and Pyramid Lakes, and that the monster serpents perhaps travel between the two bodies of water.

Regardless of whether the serpents can move between the lakes, it is true that Pyramid Lake has its legends about a sea serpent. The first modern-day mention of Pyramid's serpentine creature seems to be in an 1870 letter written by an Indian agent named Le Bass to Major Henry Douglas, Nevada Superintendent of Indian Affairs. Le Bass wrote that the Pyramid Lake Paiutes tell of their ancestors seeing a "large snake or serpent in the lake some two or three hundred feet long." Additionally, the official Paiute history (*Numa: A Northern Paiute History*, produced in 1976 by the Inter-Tribal Council of Nevada), tells an old story of two young men in their twenties who were swimming in Pyramid Lake. One of them joked with the other, saying, "What would you do if a big monster swam toward us?" The other, however, cautioned the man not to mock the lake. The respectful one swam to some rocks where the men planned to fish and climbed out of the lake. As he looked back, he saw, to his horror, a "huge monster with a large head swim toward his friend, grab his line and pull him under the water."

According to the tale, the man in the water struggled against the monster and was able to surface three times before being pulled down again. Meanwhile, his friend ran to camp to get help. A rescue party returned to the lake but found no trace of him in the lake. Sometime later, his remains were discovered—nothing was left but his head, arms, and shoulders. "It was said that the monster must have swallowed him feet first, until his arms stuck in its mouth."

Starting in the mid-twentieth century, the legends about Walker Lake's sea serpents finally caught the eye of local tourism promoters. During the past few decades, mechanical floating versions of a sea serpent, named Cecil the Sea Serpent, have popped up on the lake during various special events. Every year, a colorful, motorized sea serpent float also appears in Hawthorne's Armed Forces Day parade, one of the biggest local celebrations.

Of course, that's not to say that all serious serpent sightings have stopped. The Walker Lake Interpretative Association, a non-profit educational group with the mission of providing information about the lake, printed an e-mail from a visitor to the area named Joshua Segel on its website that read in part as follows:

On Monday June 27th, 2005, I was driving from Reno, NV, to Las Vegas, NV, on US Highway 95. Between the hours of 4 p.m.–5 p.m., my drive brought me to Walker Lake. Noticing there were no boats on the water and a sign saying Private Reservation or Reserve, I thought this to be pretty weird for such a large lake. Come to find out a few miles ahead, you are allowed to launch boats. Anyway, as I viewed the lake on my left side, with a clear view because my '95 Jeep Wrangler had the soft-top windows down, I noticed two birds sitting on the water pretty close to the shore. The water edge was about 200 ft. away and the birds were about another 100 ft. or so out on the water. What I saw next was unmistakably real as can be.

As I approached the area of these two birds, I noticed the one on the right was all the sudden gone, grabbed by something under the water without much commotion. The other bird stayed there, no water was splashed, then this large creature slipped quietly back down into the depths of the water. I thought at the time, 'what in the world could have been so large in this lake?' No sharks, whales, seals, or dolphins live in lakes, so what was it? I'm certain now I saw something similar to the Sea Serpent Legend. This creature slid back into the dark waters hoping no one saw it come out for a snack. The part I saw must have been its mouth and head area, which was grey and round. It measured at least two feet wide and more than eight feet long. I couldn't even see its body entirely. It slipped back down into the dark waters before it showed its true size. The lower part was much larger than the head or mouth area. The actual size of this thing must have been enormous! As quietly as it had come up from the deep waters, it slipped back, with no trace of it ever surfacing (except minus one waterfowl).

I have been thinking about what I saw in Walker Lake nonstop since Monday. Did I really see what I think I saw? The answer is yes! I saw something out there, something real, during the daytime and it wasn't a small glimpse or hoax, wasn't magically there and then gone, didn't vanish into thin air. There is something living in Walker Lake, much larger than any fish. All the Internet sites and people I've talked to over the phone seem to point to nothing recently being seen or published regarding Cecil the Sea Serpent or the Sea Serpent Legend. Now you do have something recent, a sighting, during the daytime by an individual who was sane and sober. Please don't discard this as a hoax or someone misinterpreting what they saw. I saw something in Walker Lake, real and alive.

What do you think?

CHAPTER 15

The Conqueror's *Curse*

The story goes that in the early 1950s, actor/director Dick Powell was developing a historical epic for RKO Pictures called *The Conqueror* based on the life (and, of course, the loves) of the legendary, twelfth-century Mongol warrior king, Genghis Khan. His original plan was to cast the currently hot young star Marlon Brando in the lead. The screenwriter, Oscar Millard, wrote the dialogue with Brando in mind, later noting, "I decided to write it in stylized, slightly archaic English. Mindful of the fact this would give it a certain cachet, I left no lily unpainted. It was a mistake I have never repeated."

Unfortunately, Brando's studio, Fox, refused to release the actor to make a picture for a competitor, so Powell was left scrambling for another lead. In early 1954, actor John Wayne had a meeting with Powell and noticed the draft script for *The Conqueror*. He glanced over the pages and asked if he could have the part because he was looking for a project that would challenge him and that would be different from the typical Westerns he had been making for years.

COURTESY OF THE DEPARTMENT OF ENERGY

The brilliant mushroom cloud of the Operation Upshot-Knothole atomic bomb explosion in 1953

Powell later recalled that he was shocked that Wayne, known as Duke, would be interested in the film. "Wayne as the barbarous Genghis Khan? I asked him if he was serious and he said he was," Powell later recalled. "We discussed the matter thoroughly, and the more we talked the more the idea intrigued me. Besides, who am I to turn down John Wayne?"

In the biography *John Wayne: American*, co-authors Randy Roberts and James Stuart Olson wrote that Powell should have talked the Western star out of taking the part because a film that was expressly written for Marlon Brando but starred John Wayne "was a disaster waiting to happen." Millard recalled that he was opposed to Wayne doing the part. "When he starts mangling those lines," he said he told Powell. "He's going to be a joke."

Cecil Adams, author of The Straight Dope column, which appeared in the *Chicago Reader* newspaper from 1973 to 2018, added, "The script was written in a cornball style that was made even more ludicrous by the Duke's wooden line readings." Adams quoted one reviewer saying that the casting of Wayne as Genghis Khan was the "most improbable piece of casting unless Mickey Rooney were to play Jesus in *The King of Kings*."

With Wayne on board, Powell cast the red-haired Susan Hayward as the Tartar princess Bortai, the object of Wayne's desire; the equally redheaded Agnes Moorehead as his mother, Hunlan; and Mexican actor Pedro Armendáriz as Jamuga, his best friend and sidekick. Needless to say, authenticity wasn't a high priority with this film, which was produced by eccentric billionaire Howard Hughes, who owned RKO at the time.

Powell selected the remote, desolate Snow Canyon in the Escalante Valley near St. George, Utah, as the site for most of the filming, which began in June of 1954. While it wasn't the Khan's native Gobi Desert, the Utah landscape was similarly harsh and unaccommodating. The heat during the day rose to nearly 120 degrees and at one point during production, a flash flood nearly wiped out the crew, sets, and equipment.

Unfortunately, a crappy script, bad acting, and an unfriendly terrain weren't the worst things the cast and crew of *The Conqueror* had to deal with. The Escalante Valley site is 137 miles downwind of the Nevada Test Site, where, between 1951 and 1992, the US government had regularly tested atomic bombs of varying sizes and strength. Adams said that the film crew was aware of the testing because a publicity photo exists of Wayne operating a Geiger counter during the filming, but the government had assured the studio that there was no danger—apparently unconcerned about the fact that the year before it had conducted 11 atmospheric nuclear tests, including "Dirty Harry," a 32-kiloton explosion on May 19, 1953, that caked the St. George area in nuclear fallout.

To make the fight scenes more authentic, huge fans were brought in to create giant sandstorms, which whipped up the irradiated dirt. Roberts and Olson wrote that "crew members were covered in dust by the end of each day's shooting, and cast members had to be frequently blown clean of dust with compressed air and given time to rinse the dirt out of their mouths and eyes. And if that wasn't enough, after the film wrapped in August, Powell trucked some 60 tons of the Utah dirt to Hollywood for reshoots. "For another two months the cast and crew wallowed in the radioactive mix," Roberts and Olson said.

Of course, at the time few were aware of the potential hazards of spending weeks exposed to unknown levels of radioactive fallout. And while no definitive link has ever been made between making the film near St. George and any type of illness, some have suggested that it is more than a coincidence that by 1981, 91 of *The Conqueror*'s 220-member cast and crew, including all of the principals, had developed some form of cancer and more than half of those had died. One of the difficulties in making such a connection is that many of the actors and crew were heavy smokers. Additionally, many of the participants didn't become sick until years, or even decades, after the movie had been made.

In 1980, however, Dr. Robert Pendleton, director of radiological health at the University of Utah, told *People* magazine, "With these numbers, this case could qualify as an epidemic." Pendleton acknowledged that a direct connection between fallout radiation and cancer is nearly impossible to prove but "in a group this size you'd expect only 30-some cancers to develop. With 91, I think the tie-in to their exposure on the set of *The Conqueror* would hold up even in a court of law."

The first member of *The Conqueror* crew to die was the director, Dick Powell, who succumbed to lung cancer on January 2, 1963, at the age of fifty-eight. Powell, who had a successful career as a television and film actor, was a heavy smoker so it was generally assumed that his nicotine habit was the primary cause of his death. But Dr. Ronald S. Oseas of Harbor UCLA Medical Center told *People*, "It is known that radiation contributes to the risk of cancer . . . with these numbers, it is highly probable that *The Conqueror* group was affected by that additive effect."

The next death was perhaps the most tragic. Actor Pedro Armendáriz was diagnosed with kidney cancer in 1959, which he seemed to beat with treatment. In June 1963, he was told the cancer was back, this time in his throat, and that he had only three months to live. After sending his wife out for a ham sandwich, the fifty-one-year-old actor picked up a pistol and shot himself in the heart. His wife later said she understood why he did it because he was facing a slow and very painful death.

In 1964, John Wayne learned that he had developed lung cancer. He embarked on aggressive treatment, including the removal of the cancerous lung, which seemed to cure him but left him short of breath. Despite the loss of a lung, however, Wayne continued to smoke several packs of cigarettes per day. The actor never blamed filming *The Conqueror* for his health problems, instead choosing to believe they were related to his smoking habit. In the late 1970s, Wayne's cancer re-emerged, this time in his stomach and remaining lung. Again, he sought treatment for the disease but ultimately lost the battle on June 11, 1979, at the age of seventy-two.

According to *People,* actress Agnes Moorehead was the first member of the cast to make the connection between the film and cancer. Apparently, in the 1960s, when she was a cast member of the TV show *Bewitched,* she told a close friend that she thought the cast had been exposed to radioactive fallout. In 1974, the curse of *The Conqueror* struck again as the seventy-three-year-old actress was diagnosed with uterine cancer. According to *People,* Moorehead later said, "Everybody in that picture has gotten cancer and died." As she lay dying, she also reportedly told friends that she never should have agreed to appear in the film.

Yet another major star to die of cancer after appearing in the film was the female lead, Susan Hayward. In March 1972, she was told she had inoperable brain cancer. For the next three years, she endured various painful treatments and therapies in an attempt to beat the cancer. On March 14, 1975, however, her body finally gave out, ravaged by cancers of the skin, breast, uterus, and brain. She was fifty-seven years old. Her son, Tim Barker, told *People* that the disease took a tremendous toll on his mother in her final days. "She was in a fetal position, she had lost her swallowing reflex, she had pneumonia, and she had lost her hair," he said.

Some cast members managed to live longer before succumbing to some form of cancer. Actress Jeanne Gerson, who had a bit part as one of Hayward's handmaidens, was first diagnosed with skin cancer in 1965. She had surgery to remove the cancerous growth and appeared to be fine for the next dozen years. But in 1977, the cancer returned in her breast. She underwent a mastectomy and had chemotherapy treatments for the next few years. The second round of cancer convinced her that it was more than coincidence that so many people involved with *The Conqueror* contracted cancer. In 1980, she hired an attorney to file a class-action suit against the federal government but nothing came of it. She died on February 7, 1992, at the age of eighty-seven—of cancer and pneumonia. Likewise, character actor John Hoyt, who had portrayed the Shaman in *The Conqueror,* lived to the ripe old age of eighty-five when he died—of lung cancer—on September 15, 1991.

It wasn't only the cast and crew of the film that were affected by the three months in the Utah desert. During filming, John Wayne's young sons, Michael and Patrick, as well as Susan Hayward's son, Tim, spent time on the set of the film. Michael and Patrick Wayne even had uncredited parts in the film. All three have had serious brushes with cancer. In 1969, Patrick had a benign breast tumor removed while Michael developed skin cancer in 1975 (in 2003, he died of heart failure as the result of lupus at the age of sixty-eight). Tim Barker had a benign tumor removed from his mouth in 1968.

And perhaps the most affected group were the people of the St. George area, now known as the downwinders. After atmospheric testing of nuclear bombs began on the Nevada site in

1951, government officials assured St. George and other communities in Iron County that there was no safety risk involved with the tests. However, following a cluster of detonations (called the Upshot-Knothole series) from March 17, 1953, to June 4, 1953, which included the massive Dirty Harry explosion, there were signs that something was amiss. In April and May of 1953, ranchers noticed burns on the skin, face, and lips of sheep that had been eating grass that later proved to be radioactive. Ewes began miscarrying in large numbers and wool literally fell off the sheep in big clumps, with visible blisters underneath. Some lambs were stillborn and had what has been described as "grotesque deformities" or were unable to nurse because they were so sickly. An estimated third of the 18,000 to 20,000 sheep in the region died.

Additionally, within five years of the tests, there was a jump in the number of people diagnosed with leukemia and radiation-related cancers in the residents of southern Utah, southeastern Nevada, and northern Arizona—all downwind of the detonations. Towns with little history of childhood leukemia suddenly had clusters of children suffering from the disease.

Despite the evidence, the US government refused to admit responsibility. According to Janet Burton Seegmiller, author of *The History of Iron County*, the Atomic Energy Commission (AEC) "chose to ignore warnings from its own scientists and outside medical researchers and continued with a 'nothing-must-stop-the-tests' rationale." Seegmiller said that an agricultural agent in the county was given a small Geiger counter to check radiation levels and found the needle went off the scale when he visited the sheep pens in Cedar City (near St. George). But after he told AEC authorities, he was instructed not to say anything because the government didn't want to be liable for paying damages to ranchers or residents.

The federal government effectively squashed any lawsuits filed in the mid-1950s. In 1979, the cases were reopened when new evidence came to light regarding the government's role in covering up the true impacts of the bomb testing. While the downwinders won in a lower court, the US Tenth Court of Appeals sided with the government, a decision the US Supreme Court refused to overturn. The Appeals Court ruled that nothing new had been presented to justify changing the original opinion. In 1990, however, Congress passed the Radiation Exposure Compensation Act and authorized the creation of a $100 million trust fund to compensate the downstate victims as well as uranium miners and test-site workers. The act was amended ten years later to drop the compensation cap, add uranium mill and ore workers, and expand the geographic region affected by fallout. To date, more than $1 billion has been paid.

Perhaps Marlon Brando was the luckiest one of all since he lost out on the part.

CHAPTER 16

The Strange Death of Adventurer Steve Fossett

I t was excellent weather for a short flight before lunch. The sky was nearly cloudless, and there was a light breeze. It should have been a piece-of-cake ride for adventurer Steve Fossett, the millionaire who, in 2002, had been the first person to circle the world alone in a balloon and who also had circumnavigated the globe in an aircraft without refueling, competed in the Iditarod dog sled race, completed an Ironman triathlon, and swam the English Channel. In fact, he personally was responsible for setting 115 world records (sixty of which still stand).

On September 3, 2007, the sixty-three-year-old Fossett and his wife, Peggy, were visiting an old friend, hotel billionaire Barron Hilton, at the latter's private, million-acre Flying M Ranch, located south of Yerington, Nevada. At about 8:30 a.m., Fossett climbed into Hilton's distinctive blue-and-white Bellanca Super Decathlon stunt plane and took off for a short ride. He didn't plan to be gone long, and he threw on a white shirt, black sweatpants, and sneakers, leaving behind his cell phone and GPS unit. His plane didn't carry a parachute and he didn't file a flight plan. He told his host that he wanted to survey the flat, dry lakebeds in the Mammoth Lakes area to find a site where he could make his next world-record attempt—breaking the land-speed record in a rocket-propelled vehicle. He planned to fly for a few hours and return in time for lunch with his wife and Hilton.

Fossett told Hilton's staff pilot, Mike Gilles, that he was going out "to play for a while." Gilles reviewed the preflight and landing procedures for the plane with the veteran pilot, then watched as the Bellanca taxied down the runway and took off. About an hour later, Rawley Bigsby, a Flying M Ranch hand, spotted the plane overhead. He had just embarked on a long road trip to Texas and Oregon and recognized the aircraft, which he had also seen a few hours earlier. The plane was flying low, about 60 to 80 feet above the ground as if the pilot were looking for a place to land. He thought the pilot was playing around, rocking the craft slightly from side to side, the tail pitching up and down. He lost sight of it as it flew over the Mud Springs area.

It was the last time anyone saw the plane.

At about noon, Fossett's wife and others at the Flying M became a little concerned when he didn't return for lunch. She didn't immediately think anything was seriously wrong because her husband was a trained pilot—and she knew he was a survivor. In 1998, while making his fourth attempt to become the first balloonist to circle the globe nonstop, his balloon had crashed into the Coral Sea about 500 miles east of Australia. Cruising at an altitude of nearly 30,000 feet, he had encountered a thunderstorm that

PHOTO BY MARY FRANCES HOWARD, COURTESY OF WWW.WICKIMEDIA.ORG

Adventurer Steve Fossett

ruptured part of his balloon and plunged his capsule into the sea. He barely escaped with his life and spent several days floating in a raft before being rescued. She also knew that he wasn't a quitter: In 2002 he tried again, this time finally succeeding in his quest to pilot a balloon around the world.

By afternoon, however, calls went out to local and state authorities, which quickly sent out several search planes. When they found no sign of Fossett, the search continued through the night with a Navy helicopter using an infrared scanner. Within days, the search party had enlarged to include more than forty-five planes at a time, all searching the Sierra Nevada and surrounding ranges for any sign of Fossett's plane.

For the next month, dozens of state and federal search and rescue crews along with hundreds of volunteers, many in their own planes, crisscrossed the mountains and deserts of western Nevada and eastern California looking for any sign of the missing aviator. Barron Hilton asked fellow aviators and friends to help, including former astronaut Neil Armstrong and Terry Delore, who had helped Fossett set ten world records in a glider. Hundreds of leads—all ultimately fruitless—came from laypeople studying updated satellite images available on Google Earth. A psychic was brought to the Flying M in mid-September but produced nothing useful. The manhunt, which cost millions of dollars and covered some 20,000 square miles, was reportedly the largest of its kind in US history. In 2008, the cash-strapped state of Nevada tried to bill Fossett's estate $687,000 for its costs but was rebuffed when Mrs. Fossett said she had spent more than $1 million of her own money on the search and maintained that search-and-rescue operations are a state responsibility. Barron Hilton, however, did contribute $200,000 to the state effort.

In early October 2007, Peggy Fossett released a statement indicating that she no longer thought her husband could be alive. The government curtailed but did not completely halt its efforts to find the missing plane, and dozens of volunteers continued their search. Mrs. Fossett, still committed to finding out what had happened to her husband, hired a team of high-tech experts to use a jet equipped with a high-resolution camera to photograph the entire search area. Those images, according to *Esquire* magazine, captured an area as large as Massachusetts and Rhode Island, and were "sharp enough to make objects as small as this magazine distinguishable." The plan was to take the ten terabytes of images and, using a special computer program, scan each pixel to identify anything that was blue, which was the color of the downed airplane. Unfortunately, it turned out there was too much blue to make sense of the images. The team found it nearly impossible to distinguish all the blue images since patches of snow showed up as blue, camping tents were blue, even handicapped parking spaces were blue.

In November 2007, Peggy Fossett asked a court in Fossett's hometown of Chicago to declare him legally dead. "As difficult as it is for me to reach this conclusion, I no longer hold out any hope that Steve has survived," she wrote in court documents. Her request was granted in February 2008.

Not surprisingly, the conspiracy theorists soon began speculating that Fossett, who was said to be worth more than $20 million (he had made his fortune as a soybean trader), had faked his own death for a variety of reasons. The London-based *Independent* newspaper wrote, "The faked death story goes as follows. In the months leading up to his death, Fossett may have been leading what breathless news reports describe as 'a secret double life.' There were suggestions that he had opened secret bank accounts and was cheating on his wife of 38 years with not one, but two mistresses. His finances had taken a hit after a string of unlucky investments, and the prospect of a messy divorce had left him facing public humiliation and financial ruin." The paper speculated that Fossett was a "born showman," and faking his death would be a fitting legacy for a man with such a theatrical flair.

Additionally, the *Independent* quoted a Chicago-based private detective, Paul Ciolino, allegedly employed by the insurance broker who claims to have sold a large life-insurance policy through Lloyd's of London to Fossett—although lawyers for Mrs. Fossett said no such policy exists. Ciolino said that things about the disappearance didn't "add up." According to the private eye, Fossett was an experienced pilot with more than a hundred land- and air-speed records, who owned every state-of-the-art electronic toy and device, yet he didn't bring any of those gadgets with him.

"The plane was crash-proof," Ciolino told the *Independent*. "Even if he'd suffered a complete engine failure, he could have guided that thing down." The detective also suggested that something was amiss regarding the haste with which Fossett was declared dead: "I deal in a lot of probate cases involving very large estates, and nothing ever happens fast in them. But that guy got declared dead in world-record time."

Others made similar suggestions. In July 2008, Lieutenant Colonel Cynthia Ryan of the US Civil Air Patrol, who was involved in the search, told the *London Telegraph* that Fossett "may have faked his own death due to personal problems or fears about his business dealings." Ryan said she had participated in search-and-rescue missions for fourteen years and "Fossett should have been found." Some Internet conspiracy buffs claimed, with no proof, that the aviator had flown south of the border and changed his identity. At least one man insisted aliens had abducted Fossett, just like in the film *Close Encounters of the Third Kind*. He suggested that alien intervention made sense since Nevada is the home of mysterious Area 51.

Articles began to appear that compared his disappearance to that of orchestra leader Glenn Miller, whose airplane was never again seen after it vanished into the London fog in 1944, and hijacker D. B. Cooper, who, in 1971, parachuted from a Boeing 727 with a $200,000 ransom and was never seen again. The *Associated Press* ran an article drawing parallels between Fossett and the mystery of Amelia Earhart's disappearance over the Pacific Ocean in 1937. In the story, Ric Gillespie, head of the International Group for Historic Aircraft Recovery, said, "We like to think that anything is findable with enough resources. But it could turn into another Amelia Earhart situation." Gillespie noted, "If they don't find something, the mystery element will grow and grow . . . if it turns into a mysterious flight into oblivion, he will be more famous than he already is." And perhaps showing prescience, he added, "If he isn't found by an aerial search, some hiker or hunter will stumble onto the wreckage some day."

On Monday, October 1, 2008, Preston Morrow was hiking with his dog, Kona, in Red's Meadow near Mammoth Mountain, California, when he stumbled across $1,005 (ten $100 bills and a $5 bill) in sun-baked notes and a faded pilot's license and other identification belonging to Steve Fossett. He told media that at first he didn't connect the stuff with Fossett. He said he thought it had been stolen from a backpack by a bear but the next morning he realized it might be Fossett's belongings. He returned to the site with his wife, some friends, and a videographer to document what he had found and to get accurate GPS coordinates to provide authorities. On Wednesday, he turned over everything he had found to local police.

Search teams were immediately dispatched to the area. Late that evening, searchers in the air and on foot located the crash site about a quarter of a mile from where Morrow had uncovered the cash and ID cards. Later, Madera County Sheriff John Anderson told the media, "The crash looked to be so severe that I doubt someone would have walked away from it." Investigators said that it appeared the airplane flew straight into a rocky mountainside and disintegrated upon impact.

In addition to finding debris from the plane strewn around the site, including the engine and a portion of the section containing its tail number, searchers discovered two bone fragments, including an oblong piece that measured 2 by 1½ inches, as well as Fossett's tennis shoes and an Illinois driver's license, both with animal bites on them. The National Transportation Safety Board (NTSB) said it believed the remains to be human but reserved judgment as to whether it was from Fossett until after a DNA test. Working quickly, authorities announced a day later that the California Department of Justice had positively identified the bones as the remains of the missing adventurer.

Experts said the reason the wreckage had not been previously seen was that it was found about 65 miles from the Flying M Ranch, slightly beyond the area in which search crews had focused their efforts. Upon receiving the news, Peggy Fossett thanked Morrow for his help in locating the plane and said the discovery would allow her to bring closure to "a very painful chapter in my life." The search of the crash site was suspended on October 5, 2008, after snow began to fall in the mountains. According to the Madera County Sheriff's Office, efforts would have to resume the following summer.

It was up to the *Times* of London to properly scold those who had earlier suggested that Fossett had faked his death. "Facts have an unfortunate habit of ruining otherwise vastly entertaining conspiracy theories," the paper said.

So what did happen to Steve Fossett? Why did an experienced pilot of his stature apparently slam his plane into the side of a mountain? Mono County, California, Undersheriff Ralph Obenberger told the *Associated Press* that he had seen large thunderheads over the Mammoth Lakes area on the day of the crash. However, Bill Manning, director of the Mammoth Yosemite Airport, speculated that Fossett could have run into trouble because he was inexperienced with the tricky winds that come off the Sierra Nevada range—the zephyrs. He said that when a pilot flies low to the mountains, like Fossett was seen doing, the updrafts and downdrafts often toss a small plane around in unexpected ways. Similarly, others talked about the range's Bermuda Triangle effect, which occurs when a pilot is hugging the mountain ridges so closely that he suddenly finds himself in a dead-end canyon, unable to pull the plane up fast enough or high enough to avoid flying into the mountain. And there are those who wonder if the adventurer suffered a heart attack while at the controls or had mechanical problems that caused the plane to lose altitude or control. In July 2009, the NTSB finally determined that the plane carrying Fossett had slammed into the mountains "following an inadvertent encounter with downdrafts that exceeded the climb capability of the airplane."

So aliens didn't abduct him?

CHAPTER 17

Who Shot Reno Casino
Owner Lincoln Fitzgerald?

I t was shortly before midnight on Saturday, November 19, 1949, when Lincoln Fitzgerald and his wife, Meta, decided to drive to the Nevada Club, the Reno casino that they co-owned. The fifty-seven-year-old Fitzgerald slowly opened the garage door, his slight frame silhouetted in the light. The cold night air—the temperature had dropped to the mid-twenties—slapped him in the face. Suddenly, from the darkness came a bright flash, immediately followed by the throaty boom of twin shotgun blasts. One shot missed but the other peppered the bespectacled casino-owner's body.

"The assailant stood so close that wadding from the shotgun shell was impacted in the gaping wound," reported the *Associated Press* the next day. "The charge, which entered his side and severed his spine, may cause his death."

The assassin immediately fled the scene after Fitzgerald's wife, who was in the bathroom, started screaming and ran from the couple's elegant home at 123 Mark Twain Avenue. Later, she told

Downtown Reno's casino row, including Lincoln Fitzgerald's Nevada Club, was a busy place in the 1950s.

reporters that her husband had made "a beautiful target" for the shooter. The *Associated Press* speculated that Fitzgerald may have seen his assailant but noted that his condition was so grave that he could not be questioned and only massive blood transfusions kept him alive. "The gunman must have hidden behind a hedge, in a dark patio, at the edge of the garage. There had been no alarm from the dog at the house next door," the wire service reported. Another account said that police thought the shooter had studied Fitzgerald's habits and patterns for a while and had found that the casino owner left for his club at about quarter to midnight nearly every night.

The *United Press* reported the shooting in a slightly more sensational style.

"In typical gangland fashion, Fitzgerald would not talk about the identity of his assailant—if he recognized him at all.

"'Do you know who shot you?' police chief Lorenz Greeson asked Fitzgerald as he lay on the operating table, still conscious.

"'No,' said Fitzgerald.

"'Was it one of the boys from Detroit?'

"Fitzgerald pursed his lips, stared at Greeson, and said nothing."

Who would have wanted to kill the casino executive and professional gambler? It's a question that has never been answered. No one was ever arrested for the shooting, which Fitzgerald managed to survive. Newspaper accounts of the day hinted that the reason Fitzgerald had been attacked was because of his long association with a Detroit-based organized-crime group commonly called the Chesterfield Syndicate (affiliated with the more well-known Purple Gang) before moving to Reno. From about 1940 to 1946, Fitzgerald and Danny Sullivan operated an illegal casino, the Chesterfield Club, in the Motor City on behalf of the syndicate. In 1946, Fitzgerald and Sullivan (who became partners in the Nevada Club) fled Michigan to avoid being prosecuted for their involvement in illegal gambling. In 1948, the two men, who had fought extradition to Michigan for two years, agreed to plead guilty to the gambling charges and pay $52,000 in fines and costs. It was thought that resolving the issue and paying the fines would allow Fitzgerald and Sullivan to put Detroit behind them once and for all.

"Gambling is legal and wide open in Nevada," said the *Associated Press*. "Reno has had no real gangster-type crimes. Old-timers remember no previous attempt of the kind on a gambler's life. Speaking of himself and Fitzgerald, [Danny] Sullivan had said, 'We're not gangsters; we're just gamblers.' Sullivan told a reporter, 'In this world, you never know who hates you. The way they are snatching babies and killing children these days, you can never tell what might happen.'"

Greeson told reporters that robbery did not appear to be the motive, even though Fitzgerald was known to carry large sums of money and frequently paid his employees in cash. The chief added that detectives were investigating former casino employees, particularly those who might have been fired, as potential suspects. In a follow-up report, the chief said that evidence, including shot removed from Fitzgerald's wounds, indicated the shooter used a sawed-off, double-barrel shotgun loaded with size 4 or size 5 shot, which is usually reserved for shooting game birds. He said that fact seemed to indicate that the gunman might be someone local, perhaps a hunter, because a professional hitman would have used heavier buckshot.

Of course, that begs the motive question: Who would have wanted to take out Fitzgerald? Some historians point out that most of the owners of Reno's gambling parlors, such as William Harrah (Harrah's Casino) and Raymond I. Smith (Harolds Club), had started out in the carnival business and were not experienced, "connected" professional gamblers, like Fitzgerald and Sullivan. There was a fear that the Detroit outsiders might seriously cut into the business of the existing clubs, and that seems to have been the case as the Nevada Club was an instant hit after it opened its doors. But nothing in either Harrah's or Smith's background would indicate any kind of involvement in such a crime. Both men had no prior record for committing or condoning violent crimes and, in fact, had established sterling reputations in Reno.

The most logical candidates were longtime Reno gangsters William Graham and James McKay, owners of the rival Bank Club and former associates of gangland killers like Baby Face Nelson. In fact, some have conjectured that Nelson himself may have been the triggerman, despite the fact he was shot to death in 1934. A website devoted to the history of Reno casinos, www.OldReno.com, theorizes, "It is no huge leap of the mind to calculate that the hit on Fitzgerald was perpetrated by a local casino owner who wanted to warn Fitz. He wanted to warn him that this was serious business, and to stay on his side of the street, and out of other people's business. The dirty little secret is that the hit was done by a Reno local to send a message to the new guy in town."

By the time Fitzgerald and Sullivan had purchased the Nevada Club in 1946, Graham and McKay, who served time in prison for mail fraud from 1939 to 1945, had just returned to operating the Bank Club. Long the kingpins of Reno's underworld, they certainly could have had a motive: resentment of the former Detroit syndicate gangsters muscling onto their turf. Given their recent stays at Leavenworth Federal Penitentiary, however, it's unlikely they would have wanted to ignite a gang war. Additionally, if two locals had committed the hit, why would a big-time organized-crime associate like Fitzgerald be so reluctant to cooperate with police or retaliate?

Despite the severity of his injuries, Fitzgerald did not die. During the next five months, while he recovered from the attack, an armed guard was stationed at all times outside his door. He was left with kidney and liver damage as well as a permanent limp. Obviously fearful that there might be another attempt on his life, Fitzgerald and his wife abandoned their home on Mark Twain Avenue and moved into quarters above the Nevada Club. The elegantly furnished apartment, which boasted a grand piano, had no windows and only a few doors so that Fitzgerald would feel safe from any enemies. Following the shooting and during the next few years, Fitzgerald and his wife were rarely seen in public and, it has been reported, did not allow any photos to be taken of them. OldReno.com notes that since the Fitzgeralds owned several Afghan hounds, they were occasionally seen in and around the Nevada Club in downtown Reno walking their dogs.

Although Fitzgerald withdrew from the public eye, he didn't disappear from Nevada's gambling industry. He was a constant presence in his casino, maintaining an active, hands-on approach to managing the property that included interviewing every new employee, counting the daily slot machine proceeds, and, often, paying employees personally. In 1952, he expanded the original casino into the adjacent Jacobs Building, and a few years later he installed a restaurant in the club—one of the first eating establishments opened inside a casino. In the late 1950s, Fitzgerald purchased the Biltmore Club on the north shore of Lake Tahoe and renamed it the Nevada Lodge. He also acquired outright ownership of the Nevada Club following Danny Sullivan's death in 1956. In the early 1960s, Fitzgerald bought the Silver Dollar Club, across Virginia Street from the Nevada Club, which he operated under that name until 1974, when it was demolished for construction of Fitzgerald's Casino and Hotel, completed two years later. The new Irish-themed resort, built during a miniboom in Reno casino construction in the early '70s, boasted a sixteen-story, 347-room hotel, more than 1,000 slot machines, two restaurants, and a small lounge for live entertainment. Records indicate that Fitzgerald paid for construction of the $16 million property in cash.

While the casino owner was able to beat the odds when it came to an assassin's bullets, he couldn't defeat the march of time. On April 18, 1981, Fitzgerald died at the age of eighty-eight. His wife contemplated continuing to manage the properties but decided, at age sixty-nine and in poor health, to turn them over to someone else to operate. About two years after her husband's death, Meta Fitzgerald leased her holdings to a group of veteran casino executives known as Lincoln Management Group. In 1986, she sold all of her casino interests to the company.

An interesting side note is that following the sale, Meta Fitzgerald moved from the secure apartment above the Nevada Club into a Reno retirement home. After her departure, the new owners found that she had left behind the grand piano, which was too large to be removed via the stairs or elevator. Apparently, the piano had been brought upstairs through large windows in the Douglas Alley (behind the casino) using a crane, but those openings had been bricked up for security reasons following the attempt on Lincoln Fitzgerald's life. It was only after removing the bricks that the substantial musical instrument could be moved. Meta Fitzgerald lived in Reno until the late 1990s, when she returned to Michigan to be closer to family. She died in March 2004 at ninety-two.

Who tried to kill Lincoln Fitzgerald? The more or less official conclusion was that somehow he had fallen into disfavor with his old cronies in Detroit, who had put out a contract on his life. Some have suggested that he may have skimmed some money off the Chesterfield Club just prior to splitting from Detroit for Reno. There are even rumors that following the shooting, Fitzgerald not only didn't cooperate with the investigation but also used his influence to quash the case because he didn't want to push his luck. Reno's police authorities didn't appear too certain that they were ever going to solve the crime when, a few months after the attack, one predicted that the case would likely end up being just like the shooting death of gangster Benjamin "Bugsy" Siegel two years earlier—just another unsolved gangland hit.

In 1950, during hearings before the Senate Special Committee to Investigate Organized Crime in Interstate Commerce, Virgil W. Peterson, operating director of the Chicago Crime Commission, presented a comprehensive history of organized-crime syndicates throughout the country and stated, "Lincoln Fitzgerald, next to [Mert] Westheimer, was the most powerful member of the Chesterfield syndicate in Michigan. . . . Lincoln Fitzgerald and Daniel Sullivan became fugitives from Michigan, where they were under indictment. They finally went back to Michigan and paid fines and costs totaling $52,000. While they were fugitives they became the owners and operators of the Nevada Club, one of the most important Reno gambling establishments."

Perhaps adding a postscript to the Fitzgerald shootings, he continued: "About midnight on November 18, 1949, as Lincoln Fitzgerald was leaving his home in Reno for the Nevada Club, he was ambushed and shot. At first his condition was thought to be critical. However, he recovered. Following the shooting of Fitzgerald two of the individuals under suspicion by the authorities were members of the old Purple Gang of Detroit."

As for Fitzgerald's gambling empire, the first casualty was the Nevada Lodge, which closed in the late 1980s. By the early 1990s, Lincoln Management had become overwhelmed by its own debt (it had purchased a casino-hotel in downtown Las Vegas and acquired onetime rival Harolds Club in Reno, as well as casinos in Blackhawk, Colorado, and Tunica, Mississippi) and was forced to sell the Nevada Club and Harolds Club to Harrah's, which eventually razed both of the historic casinos for an outdoor special events plaza. Lincoln Management filed for bankruptcy protection in 2000, and its various properties were liquidated over the next few years. In December 2008, Fitzgerald's Casino and Hotel, which had been sold to L3 Development Company, was closed for good. The new owners said they planned to replace it with a boutique hotel that would have shops, restaurants, and convention space—but no gambling.

As an old-time gambler—who'd almost given his life for his business—Lincoln Fitzgerald would no doubt not approve.

CHAPTER 18

Why Did Thriving Metropolis
Turn into a Ghost Town?

I t was the fall of 1912 and it had been an excellent year in the
newly established community of Metropolis. The yield on local
wheat and sugar beet crops was better than average, and work had
begun on the new two-story concrete and brick Lincoln School,
a building that would say to the world that Metropolis was a substantial town with substantial people. The new three-story Hotel
Metropolis, which had cost an impressive $100,000 (or nearly
$2.5 million today), had opened earlier in the year and it already
had guests in more than half of its rooms. And the just-completed
8-mile-long railroad spur that connected to the Southern Pacific
Railroad line just below Wells, Nevada, was bringing in more new
people every week. The town boasted more than seven hundred residents and was already one of the larger settlements in Elko County.
There was even talk of carving out a new county, with, naturally,
Metropolis as the county seat.

No one suspected it was all about to end.

Unlike nearly all of Nevada's other ghost towns, Metropolis wasn't built from the proceeds of gold or silver mines but rather on the backs of farmers, nearly all of whom had been lured to the area by promises of good, arable land, a temperate year-round climate, a more-than-adequate water supply, and ready markets in Nevada's booming mining camps.

Metropolis, however, turned out to be a mirage in the desert—a classic American land scam. The story of the community can be traced to 1909, when the Pacific Reclamation Company and the Metropolis Land Improvement Company were formed by Harvey Pierce of Leominster, Massachusetts, to develop 40,000 acres located about 17 miles northwest of Wells in the southern part of Elko County. Pierce and his staff crafted a slick promotional campaign that was long on hyperbole and, perhaps, short on complete honesty. Posters, brochures, and plentiful newspaper advertisements were filled with too-good-to-be-true claims about the area's fabulously fertile soil, lengthy growing season, and abundant water. The company predicted the planned community would eventually house 7,500 people and have convenient rail transportation. At least the part about the rail service turned out to be true for a time.

Pacific Reclamation specifically targeted Mormon farmers in Utah, even opening an office in Salt Lake City. In his book, *Old Heart of Nevada: Ghost Towns and Mining Camps of Elko County*, Nevada historian Shawn Hall recounted how the Church of Jesus Christ of Latter-day Saints (Mormon Church) "encouraged people to move to Metropolis, and during the summer of 1911 a steady flow of them began to arrive. About 95 percent of the Metropolis population was Mormon." In fact, quarter-page advertisements

This giant brick and stone arch is just about all that remains of Lincoln School in the once-bustling agricultural community of Metropolis.

placed in Utah newspapers at the time proclaimed "Metropolis is the Place" in large text—an obvious attempt to mirror the words of Mormon Church leader Brigham Young, who said, "This is the place" when he arrived in the valley at the base of Utah's Wasatch Range with his followers in 1847 and established Salt Lake City.

Large ads placed in the two Reno newspapers, the *Reno Evening Gazette* and the *Nevada State Journal*, where the company maintained its other office, appeared regularly in 1911 and 1912. In the *Journal*, Metropolis's developer advertised a contest in the winter of 1911 with "$400 in Real Estate Given Away." According to the ad, the contest winner would receive two lots located two blocks from the new Hotel Metropolis "in the heart of one of the richest and most fertile agriculture districts in the west." Interestingly, no details were included on how to actually enter the contest.

Another ad, which appeared almost weekly in the *Gazette* for more than four months in the spring of 1912, carried a giant headline asking, "Have You Purchased a Lot at Metropolis, Nevada?" and the text painted an enticing portrait of an agrarian paradise that "is attracting more attention than any new agricultural town in the West." The advertisement noted the new hotel was "a model of modern comfort" and "the finest hostelry in the state." It added that Metropolis offered the investor, builder, merchant, and professional man "the greatest business opportunities ever offered in a new western farming community and we urge those who contemplate making a good investment to investigate the town lot opportunities at Metropolis at once."

To support this aggressive land promotion, Pacific Reclamation constructed the Bishop Creek Dam on a tributary of the

Humboldt River to provide a reliable source of water to the farming community. The 100-foot-high dam, said to have cost $200,000, was located about 15 miles north of the town site, so the company also had to build a road leading to it. The dam itself was fabricated using some 6.5 million broken bricks transported to the site from San Francisco (taken from the ruins of buildings after the disastrous 1906 earthquake). With the completion of the dam in April 1911, the company intensified its efforts to sell its lots and farm sites. Dry farm land was priced at $10 to $15 per acre while irrigated land was $75 an acre. Town lots ranged from $100 to $300. The company claimed that it had enough water stored at Bishop Creek Dam to irrigate 10,000 acres, with plans to extend the irrigation system to an even larger area "with a corresponding development of water."

The company also established a town newspaper, called the *Metropolis Chronicle*, to promote the community's many fine attributes. The first issue, dated September 15, 1911, proclaimed on the front page, "Great Future for Metropolis," and listed all the impressive projects under construction and future developments. At the bottom of the front page was a photo depicting a lush field of wheat that was captioned: "Wheat crop averaging 45 bushels to the acre grown on dry farm land near Metropolis. Nothing but sagebrush grew on this land a year ago." Another story spoke of the Southern Pacific Railroad laying tracks to town while another, "Utah Men Buy Land," described how dozens of Utah and Idaho farmers were purchasing tracts of irrigated and dry farm land because of its desirability. Under the headline, "Fine Crop Report," the paper reported, "Smith Brothers of the Centerville Nursery in Utah have made a report in which they state that the fruit crop in the sections near Metropolis show practically full crops with losses comparatively slight, and so well pleased are they with conditions in this section of the country that they have expressed their intention of operating a branch nursery near Metropolis." The paper was mailed to prospective customers all over the country.

As new residents flocked to the community, the company laid out a town site—streets were named after US presidents—and began construction of several buildings including the fifty-room Hotel Metropolis, as well as a wooden Meeting Hall that also served as a church, theater, and gymnasium (and later as a school). The hotel was an elegant brick structure that was considered the finest hotel between Reno and Salt Lake City when it opened on December 29, 1911. Among its amenities were private baths, electric lighting, telephone service, and an elevator. On the first floor were a barbershop, a bank, a general store, and an apothecary. A few months after the hotel opened, the railroad completed a fine, two-story wooden depot with a flower garden and a water fountain, which seemed designed to reinforce the idea that Metropolis was an oasis in the desert.

Metropolis's future certainly looked bright well into the following year. A two-story stucco schoolhouse opened, and the water system was completed from the dam to town. Fire hydrants were installed throughout the four-block business district, and the company poured concrete sidewalks so residents would no longer have to wade through muddy streets. Several businesses cropped up in the town center, including several stores, a wagon company, a bank, a drugstore, and saloons. Additionally, a post office opened (in November 1911), a firehouse had been built, two small city parks were created, telephone service was initiated, and a racetrack was established.

The February 25, 1912, *Nevada State Journal* published a lengthy article proclaiming: "Metropolis Now Full Grown Town" in the headline with the subheading, "All Modern Improvements Make City of the Desert Mecca for the Opportunist." In the opening paragraph, the paper noted, "The new city of Metropolis over in eastern Elko County on the Southern Pacific railway, is advancing at a rate that is outdoing anything in like development ever before attempted in the arid West." The article noted that about seventy-five families had moved into Metropolis in the previous forty days.

"These people without one dissenting voice say that their investments in their lands have proven to be more profitable than had reason to believe," the paper said with enthusiasm. "The improvements in the last sixty days seem almost beyond reason . . . all of these wonderful situations are directly due to the good quality of the land and to the energy and resources of the men connected with the company in building the large dam and canals."

Accenting this positive press was the news, published in the *Wells Herald* in May 1912, that "Last Saturday, to mark the completion of the big dam of the Pacific Reclamation company in Emigrant canyon, a bottle of champagne was broken over the face of the dam, a speech being made later on."

However, just a month later, the Pacific Reclamation Company received devastating news. A group of thirty downstream ranchers and farmers in the Lovelock Valley had filed a lawsuit arguing that the company was illegally withholding water behind the Bishop Creek Dam that rightly belonged to them. In the suit, they claimed Pacific Reclamation had neglected to file for water rights and had improperly impounded water when it built Bishop Creek Dam. For the next three years, the farmers and the development company sparred in court. On June 15, 1915, District Court Judge E. A. Ducker of Winnemucca issued a final decree that ended the litigation. In his order, Judge Ducker sided with the Lovelock Valley interests and Pacific Reclamation was ordered to lower the water levels behind the dam so that there was only enough to provide the town with water and to irrigate 4,000 acres.

The impact of the decision was catastrophic on Pacific Reclamation and, ultimately, Metropolis. The company went into receivership and the community lost its biggest developer and benefactor. While the ornate Lincoln School, already under construction when the water rights issue flared up, was completed at a cost of $25,000, it was the last major construction project in the town. Before the year was over, the Hotel Metropolis had closed and the *Metropolis Chronicle* ceased publication.

Then came the fury of Mother Nature. During the community's first two years, Metropolis's winter and spring had been unusually wet, providing plenty of water for crops. In 1914, however, the region entered a multi-year dry period, which, it turned out, was more normal and typical for the area. In response, many farmers switched to less water-intensive crops, such as dry farm wheat, which showed promise. In 1917, when that year's wheat crop was described by many farmers as "the greatest in the history of that state," hordes of jackrabbits and squirrels appeared to chow down on the wheat crop. "The rabbits swarmed on to the field and in ten days have eaten and destroyed fully seventy-five percent of the crops leaving only the wheat in the center of the field still standing," noted the *Reno Evening Gazette* on August 17, 1917. "Horses and cattle have been turned into many of the fields now to eat what little of the crops there is left and unless the state and biological bureau come to the aid of the farmers this fall and poison the rabbits many ranchers will move away is the claim of Mr. Wiley [W. M. Wiley, manager of the Metropolis irrigation project] and the others."

A year later, in a story with the headline, "Rabbits Are Still Menace in Elko County," the *Gazette* noted that despite the best efforts of the federal and state governments and local ranchers, the rabbit and squirrel infestation remained a serious problem for Metropolis farmers. A follow-up story in the January 11, 1919, issue of the *Gazette* added an interesting spin on the problem. In a story headlined, "Killing Rabbits New Industry," the newspaper said that killing jackrabbits had become a profitable business and one of the chief industries in Metropolis. "In three months over 5,000 of the bunnies were killed," the article said. "The rabbits brought an average of fifteen cents each, and the daily sum realized [for the hunters] was $18 per day."

Additionally, the prolonged drought brought another kind of pest, the Mormon Cricket, a large, dark-colored, omnivorous insect that will consume nearly anything in its path, including crops, paint from houses, and so on. While always present in western rangelands, the crickets are thought to swarm in huge numbers during particularly dry weather conditions. In Metropolis, massive hordes of the nasty bugs descended on the community and finished off whatever crops might have survived the earlier onslaughts by rabbits and squirrels.

Not surprisingly, as these problems persisted farms began to go belly up. Farmers had tried to switch to raising dairy cows and dry farming but the rabbits and crickets usually wiped out any crops. By 1916, only a handful of farms remained in Metropolis. The loss of the farms spelled the end of nearly all of the town's non-agricultural businesses. As if all of that wasn't enough to torment residents, a typhoid epidemic broke out in February 1916, which killed a number of people, and was followed by the 1918 national influenza outbreak that also took the lives of several locals.

Eleanor Hasenkamp Holland, a teacher in Metropolis from 1917 to 1922, maintained a written and photographic record of life in the community. She told of a social scene that included dances in the dining room of the Hotel Metropolis and local plays in the Meeting House, which also doubled as the school. Life wasn't easy and everyone, including the children, had to chip in when the crops were ready. "Potato harvest was so vital that school was dismissed for a week so the youngsters could help," she wrote. "The first year, I planned to spend the week in Deeth with my college roommate who was teaching there. [The Land Company Manager] Hatch said the teachers ought to donate some help with the harvest and if we'd work two days, he'd take me to Deeth and come after me. So, we nearly killed ourselves, actually picking more potatoes than the men did."

Holland's photos from those years depict a still-thriving community with neat, tidy homes, fields filled with rows of crops and farm equipment, and impressive buildings like the hotel, train depot, small brick schoolhouse, and the larger Lincoln School. On a photo showing three smiling children eating on a large stack of wood, she noted, "Sagebrush helped out for fuel at the little old schoolhouse. The youngsters loved to play around on it, and it was a favorite lunch room on nice days."

By the early 1920s, however, only about a hundred people were still living in Metropolis and the surrounding farms. The town struggled through the next two decades. The railroad gave up in 1925, closing the depot with its beautiful flower gardens and fountain, and ripping up the tracks. By then, the vacant hotel had been severely vandalized; even its hardwood floors had been removed. A few years later, the meeting hall burned to the ground (the town's water system had fallen into such disrepair there was no water to put out the fire and save the building).

In 1936, another fire destroyed what remained of the hotel. Six years later, the post office had so little business that it, too, closed. In 1943, the magnificent Lincoln School was closed and three years later it was dismantled so the bricks could be sold off. All that remained were the solid concrete floors and an elaborately decorated concrete arch entrance. In 1949, the grammar school was closed when the district, suffering from declining enrollment, consolidated with the nearby town of Wells.

Since then, the rest of Metropolis's buildings have either been recycled for use elsewhere or disintegrated into the desert. In 1954, interest in the community was briefly rekindled when the Gulf Oil Company began leasing mineral rights from local ranchers and farmers to conduct test drilling for oil. Despite probing more than a mile deep into the ground, the company reported only trace amounts of petroleum, and the effort was quickly abandoned.

Today, not much remains of Nevada's first master-planned community. The Bishop Creek Dam still stands, and periodically there has been talk of reconstructing it to provide irrigation to nearby ranches. In 2002, the Humboldt River Basin Water Authority explored the possibility of acquiring the dam and rebuilding it for water storage but lost interest after visiting the dam site and seeing how much work would need to be done to make it useful. An article in the *Elko Daily Free Press* noted that members of the authority were disappointed the dam wasn't bigger and believed there were better sites along the Humboldt where it would be easier and cheaper to store water.

About half a dozen homesteads are still active in the area and trace their roots to the Metropolis development. There are also two cemeteries, one on a small hill east of the town center and a larger one west of the former site of the Lincoln School. Both are still tended by locals. Wandering the former downtown section, visitors can find the foundations of the old Hotel Metropolis, including a large, now-empty vault that was once used by a bank inside the hotel. Perhaps the most iconic ruin from Metropolis's glory days is the large concrete entrance of the Lincoln School, which still stands tall in a valley of low-lying sagebrush and wild grass. The distinctive arch is now dimpled with bullet holes and its ninety-year-old concrete is starting to crumble from years of neglect and exposure to the harsh elements.

In 1989, about 150 former residents and their descendants dedicated a permanent memorial to the town. The stone and concrete monument included a display with historic photos and a map of the original town site. Additionally, a bronze plaque, entitled "Remember Metropolis," asked visitors to cherish the efforts of the town's hardy pioneers and noted "many who lived here aspired to become teachers, lawyers, civic leaders, church leaders, and best of all reared great families in homes where love and happiness filled their lives . . . Blessed be the name of Metropolis, Nevada through the eternities."

An interesting postscript to the Metropolis story is that in the fall of 2008, visitors to the town of Almere, Netherlands, found a remarkable sight in a grassy lot in the town center—an exact replica of the Lincoln School archway constructed of plywood and high-resolution photographs printed on self-adhesive vinyl. The duplicate arch, called "Reclamation," was the work of American artist Kristin Posehn, who prepared it for the Museum de Paviljoens. In addition to the full-scale image of the decaying arch—which included chipped bricks, cracks, and bullet holes—Posehn's exhibit featured reprints of front pages of the *Metropolis Chronicle*, newspaper advertisements that promoted Metropolis, and the original pamphlet used to entice potential buyers. It also had contemporary and historic photos of the town as well as copies of the original architect's drawing of the Lincoln School. The Metropolis arch art project was displayed for about three months before being taken down.

Metropolis may be gone, but it is certainly not forgotten.

CHAPTER 19

Suicide or Something Else? The Mysterious Death of Raymond Spilsbury

R aymond H. Spilsbury, co-owner of the Boulder Dam Hotel and former general manager of the Cerro de Pasco Copper Corporation of Peru, drowned in the Colorado River on January 19, 1945. Those are the known facts. What isn't so certain is whether the fifty-six-year-old businessman carefully removed his coat, hat, and a wallet containing a $12,000 check made out to him along with more than $1,000 in travelers checks and about $50 in cash, placed those items in a neat pile (held down by a large, flat stone) on the bank of the river, filled his pants pockets with rocks, tied his feet together with his own belt, and flung himself into the river—as authorities ultimately decided when they declared his death a suicide—or if something else happened?

His widow, Vona A. Spilsbury, never quite accepted the official story and for the rest of her life (she died in 2001) believed there were unanswered questions surrounding her husband's death. In his book *Midnight on Arizona Street: The Secret Life of the*

BOULDER DAM HOTEL, BOULDER CITY, NEVADA

This postcard image is of the Boulder Dam Hotel in 1936, two years after it opened. The hotel was owned by Raymond Spilsbury, a successful businessman who died under mysterious circumstances in 1945.

RICHARD MORENO COLLECTION

Boulder Dam Hotel, historian Dennis McBride, who interviewed Vona Spilsbury in the 1980s, quoted her as saying, "Foul play was uppermost in our minds when we were unable to find him or his body . . . I was always suspicious of Ray's death."

So who was Raymond Spilsbury?

Raymond Harold Spilsbury was born to a wealthy Utah ranching family in Toquerville, Utah, in 1888. While the family's primary enterprise was the Spilsbury Land and Livestock Company, Spilsbury, who graduated with a science and engineering degree from the University of Utah in 1914, was more interested in metallurgy. Shortly after graduating, he took a position as a chemist for the Cerro de Pasco Copper Corporation, a large mining operation in Peru owned by an American syndicate that included

179

J. P. Morgan, Henry Clay Frick, and the Vanderbilt family. Over the next decade and a half, Spilsbury moved up in the company, becoming chief chemist, then smelter foreman, smelter superintendent, and eventually general manager.

During his early years in Peru, Spilsbury worked at Cerro de Pasco with Paul Stewart "Jim" Webb, a contractor who specialized in building lavish homes in Beverly Hills in the late 1920s. In 1931, Webb bid for a government contract to build houses in the brand-new planned community of Boulder City, which the federal government had created to house workers on the massive Boulder Dam project (later renamed Hoover Dam). He was awarded a permit to establish the Boulder City Builders Supply, a lumber and concrete block manufacturing yard outside of the town, which would supply the materials used to construct nearly all of the community's earliest structures, including the Boulder Dam Hotel.

Webb, who has been described by Vona Spilsbury as a man of tremendous vision but no finances, envisioned Boulder City as growing into a bustling resort community that would serve as the gateway to the country's newest recreational area, Lake Mead, which was being created by the waters of the Colorado River as they backed up behind Boulder Dam. In 1933, Webb sought permission from the US Bureau of Reclamation, which controlled Boulder City, to build a first-class hotel in the community. Unable to finance his dream alone, he looked for financial partners among his friends and associates, including his former Cerro de Pasco associate, Raymond Spilsbury, with whom he had previously partnered on several construction projects.

Intrigued by the idea, Spilsbury quickly agreed to form a hotel corporation with Webb and another friend from their time in Peru, Austin Clark. Webb was named president of the new venture, known as the Hotel Holding Corporation, and was placed in charge of building the hotel while Spilsbury returned to Peru. Ground was broken on the project in September 1933 and construction was completed in mid-December. The two-story stucco hotel, built in a Dutch Colonial style, featured a modern cooling and heating system, and had thirty-three rooms, each with a private bath or shower. A year later, Webb borrowed additional money from new partners in order to expand the hotel, adding a second wing that included thirty more guest rooms and a dining room. Additionally, the hotel gained an enclosed grassy terrace with a goldfish pond, fountain, and garden.

By 1936, Webb had decided the only way to grow his business was to merge—apparently without Spilsbury's knowledge—with another local tourism business, Grand Canyon-Boulder Dam Tours (GCBDT), owned by aviator and entrepreneur Glover E. "Roxie" Ruckstell. The two were convinced that the new dam and lake were sure-fire attractions that would ensure the success of their combined operations. They signed an exclusive twenty-year agreement with the National Park Service, agreeing to build, own, and operate all tourist concessions within the Lake Mead Recreation Area.

According to Dennis McBride, who has written extensively on Boulder City and Hoover Dam, during much of 1936 and the beginning of 1937, the GCBDT rapidly expanded its operations and, in doing so, attracted additional financial investors including Stewart Linden, a steel millionaire, Henry Belden, a San Francisco socialite and playboy, and Las Vegas businessman Jim Cashman. The company owned or controlled the Boulder Dam Hotel, Murl Emery's commercial boating operation, Grand Canyon Airlines, a limousine service, and the Bullock Field airport in Boulder City.

The park service deal, however, ultimately proved to be disastrous for the company. Park Service officials' demands for more regular flights to the canyon and boat tours of the lake as well as heavy investments in infrastructure, such as upgrading the airport, and a steep profit-sharing formula resulted in large financial losses for the enterprise. Despite attracting an impressive array of movie celebrities, politicians, foreign royalty, and the wealthy during the first few years—ranging from Shirley Temple and her parents to Crown Prince Olav of Norway and Crown Princess Martha—the hotel was unable to meet its debt obligations and subsidize the other money-losing parts of the company, which included the airline and airport operations.

In a 1984 article about GCBDT for the *Nevada Historical Quarterly*, McBride tells an insightful anecdote about the company's financial troubles told to him by Elton Garrett, Boulder City's first newspaper reporter: "I rode with Murl Emery in one of the boats on the lake, and saw him point up to one of the GCBDT planes flying over. He said, 'You know why we're going broke? Gasoline for those planes—they don't have enough passengers to take care of the costs.'"

In 1939, Webb severed his ties with GCBDT, but by then the financial drain on the hotel had taken a toll. Two years later, he persuaded Raymond Spilsbury's brother, Chauncey and his wife, Dolly, to relocate from Arizona to manage the struggling hotel.

Despite some initial success in turning around the property's fortunes, Chauncey and Dolly Spilsbury were unable to overcome the economic slump that followed America's entrance into World War II and the hotel became even more the worse for wear. In 1942, Webb and Spilsbury decided to dissolve their partnership, with Webb taking a lumber yard and hardware store owned by the corporation and Spilsbury assuming majority ownership of the hotel, which continued to be managed by his brother and sister-in-law (who were accepting equity in the hotel in lieu of salaries).

In mid-1944, Raymond Spilsbury retired from his mining position in the mountains of Peru, largely for health reasons. Feeling the effects of some three decades of living in high altitude, he had suffered a minor stroke a year earlier and developed angina. He and his wife relocated to Boulder City to help him regain his health and with plans to revitalize the hotel. The Provo, Utah, *Sunday Herald* reported on December 3 that Spilsbury had recently presented Brigham Young University with a check for $100 to be used to purchase books to enlarge the Roselia Haight Spilsbury collection of books on home economics in the BYU library. "The collection, which now numbers approximately 600 volumes, was established in honor of Mrs. Spilsbury by her sons and daughters," noted the paper.

* * *

In the late afternoon of Friday, January 19, 1945, despite the cold weather, Raymond Spilsbury drove alone to Emery's Landing, a small resort on Lake Mead at the mouth of the El Dorado Canyon that was about 20 miles south of Boulder City. The landing, which included a boat launch, campground, general store, and fish and bait shop, was named for and owned by Murl Emery, a legendary local boatman who had helped the federal government's engineers locate the eventual site for Boulder Dam and who managed a tour boat operation on the river. It was said that Emery, who was also an avid prospector, knew every cave, canyon, cove, and current on the Colorado. According to McBride, Emery had also lost a considerable amount of money, which he had invested in the GCBDT partnership, and may have harbored some resentment against those who had fared better after the company went bankrupt, such as Webb and Spilsbury.

In his testimony, E. H. Emery, father of Murl Emery, and the only witness to speak to Spilsbury at the landing, said the hotelier arrived at the park at about 1:30 p.m. or 2:00 p.m. He parked his blue Pontiac, climbed out of the car, locked the doors, and walked southward on a trail that paralleled the Colorado River. No other campers or visitors to the park reported seeing Spilsbury again, but several guests reported noticing his car that evening and thought it belonged to a fisherman who had not yet returned.

Murl Emery, who had been out on the river, didn't return until late that evening. He later told police that he, too, had spotted the car, which he didn't recognize. He said he tried to read the driver's license, which he could see was still inside the car, but it was turned upside down. Concerned, he rousted his wife and two of his children as well as several campers to help him search the property for the car's missing owner. Despite searching the area on foot and even taking a skiff out on the river to take a quick look, he found nothing.

The next morning, according to the January 23, 1945 issue of the *Boulder City News*, Emery's wife discovered Spilsbury's dark green dress coat and gray hat "neatly placed on a large rock underneath an overhanging boulder. A flat rock had been placed on top. The coat and hat were wet from the rain, except where partly protected by the overhang. Cards in the side pocket of the coat carried Spilsbury's name." Additionally, according to the paper, the pockets of the coat contained a check made out to Spilsbury in the amount of $12,352.40, a bank statement, fourteen travelers checks of $50 each and four of $100 each, $53 in cash, a Nevada driver's license, business cards, two pairs of glasses (one dark), and keys to rooms in the Boulder Dam Hotel.

The following day, the United Press reported that authorities were combing the banks of the Colorado River searching for Spilsbury's body. The wire service said it was feared Spilsbury "may have died from a plunge into the swirling river." On January 25, the *Boulder City News* noted that the search had shifted downstream to a site near where Davis Dam is now located (above the present-day city of Laughlin, Nevada), where authorities had established a search camp.

The manhunt continued for another five weeks, with searchers looking along the river as far south as Needles, California. Sometime during that period, Vona Spilsbury told McBride that Murl Emery approached her and "tried to blackmail me into a sum of money if he found Ray's body." But, she added, her attorney advised her not to pay the ransom, so she ignored the request.

Finally, on Monday, February 26, three fishermen from Los Angeles who were camping on the river about eight miles downstream from El Dorado Canyon spotted an arm sticking out from a clump of bushes on the edge of the river. The fishermen reported their discovery to local authorities and when the body was fished out of the river the following day by Murl Emery, it was positively identified as Raymond Spilsbury. Authorities were surprised to find that Spilsbury's ankles were tied together with his own belt and his pant pockets were stuffed with rocks. The United Press reported on February 28 that authorities believed Spilsbury, "who had been in ill health, committed suicide."

A day later, on March 1, an inquest was held in Boulder City and several of his friends and associates were asked to testify to a coroner's jury on Spilsbury's mental and physical health at the time of the incident. According to the records, a friend, Dick Webb, brother of Paul Webb, described Spilsbury as "tired" and "not physically himself." He said since arriving in Boulder City and taking a more direct hand in the hotel's operations, Spilsbury had worked "day and night." But, according to Webb, on the day of his disappearance Spilsbury "seemed to be more like himself . . . he didn't seem depressed."

E. H. Emery, the last person to see Spilsbury alive, was asked to describe their interaction on January 19 and told authorities he had only spoken to Spilsbury briefly. "He came down and talked to me and asked for Murl. I told him Murl was down the river and would not be back until evening. He said he would wait around . . . he asked me about the trail down the river. He said 'I think I will walk down there and kill time.' That was the last time I saw him." The older Emery also said Spilsbury acted normal but was a bit anxious to see his son, although he didn't indicate why he wanted to see him.

Spilsbury's brother, Chauncey, told the jurors that his brother had returned from Peru "almost a physical wreck." He said his brother had considerable pain in one of his shoulders and one leg hurt so badly that he dragged it when he walked. "During November and December we were often in conversation and I had time to learn he was ill, not only physically ill but he had lost a great deal of his mental grip," Chauncey testified. "He did not seem to retain conversations he had the day before or be able to make decisions. He seemed to have an obsession of fear of the future. What it was we did not know."

In the end, the jury ruled Spilsbury had "come to his death by his own hand" and the case was closed. Interestingly, the three-member coroner's jury consisted of local citizens including Arthur N. Minish, an engineer for the National Park Service, James W. Lytle of Boulder City, and Murl Emery, the same man Spilsbury was trying to reach on the day he took his own life, who been an active participant in the search for Spilsbury's body and who sought to extract a reward from Vona Spilsbury in return for finding her husband's body.

Immediately following the close of the inquest, Spilsbury's body was released to a Las Vegas funeral home, with memorial services performed that same evening. The remains were shipped to Forest Lawn Cemetery in Glendale, California, for cremation. A few months later, the *Salt Lake City Tribune* reported that an appraisement of Raymond Spilsbury's estate had been filed in Utah's Third District Court. According to the brief item, Spilsbury left behind an estate valued at $237,313.41 (worth about $3.3 million in 2018 dollars), comprising cash, stocks, bonds, and securities. The heirs of the estate were his widow, Vona Adeline Spilsbury, and a young son also named Raymond Harold Spilsbury.

After gaining control of her husband's assets, Vona Spilsbury discovered that a portion of the hotel's ownership shares, formerly held by Austin Clark, had been sold over the years to seven different people. She and her attorney quickly tracked down the minority owners and acquired those interests so that the Spilsbury family could have complete control of the hotel's ownership. Early in 1946, the hotel was listed for sale, and a few months later was sold to Las Vegas judge Cliff Jones, businessman Marion Hicks, and lawyers Lou Weiner Jr. and Harvey Dickerson. The price was $225,000.

Was Raymond Spilsbury's death a suicide? Despite Vona Spilsbury's claim that Murl Emery had tried to extort money from her during the time her husband was missing, and Emery losing his investment in GCBDT when that company failed, the official investigation was closed with the finding that Spilsbury killed himself. In a recent interview, author Dennis McBride said while he could never find definitive proof that Emery had anything to do with Spilsbury's death, he has long felt authorities may have closed the case a bit too hastily.

"There is one thing that is the most likely reason that Murl might have had to be angry with Spilsbury, and that was the Grand Canyon-Boulder Dam Tour Company," McBride said. "Murl Emery put a great deal of his own money into it and he lost it all. Whether that was enough to make him want to kill Spilsbury, I don't know."

McBride said aspects of the alleged suicide remain open questions, such as why was Spilsbury so eager to speak to Murl Emery on the day he disappeared into the Colorado River? And how did Spilsbury, who reportedly had a bum shoulder and could barely walk, manage to tie his feet together with his own belt and then toss himself into the Colorado River? McBride also thought there was something peculiar about where the body was found, only eight miles downstream from Emery's Landing. He said at that time the current of the Colorado, still mostly untamed by dams, was extremely strong so it's likely the body would have been carried much farther downstream.

"I do feel there's more to this story than we'll ever know," he said.

BIBLIOGRAPHY

A CHILLING DEATH

Glad, Betty. *Key Pittman: The Tragedy of a Senate Insider*. New York: Columbia University Press, 1986.

Israel, Fred. *Nevada's Key Pittman*. Lincoln, NE: University of Nebraska Press, 1963.

"National Affairs: Turn of the Wheel," *Time* magazine, November 18, 1940.

Reid, Ed, and Ovid Demaris, *The Green Felt Jungle*. New York: Trident Press, 1963.

Rocha, Guy Louis. "The Mysterious Demise of Key Pittman," *Nevada Magazine*, October 1996.

———. "Key Pittman on Ice," Myth #3, Nevada Historical Myth of the Month, www.nevadaculture.org.

AT THE BOTTOM OF LAKE TAHOE

Close, Alex. "Myths and Legends of Tahoe," *Sierra Sun*, December 29, 2006.

James, George Wharton. *The Lake in the Sky. Boston:* L.C. Page & Co. Boston Publishers, 1921.

Louise, Cherie. "Who Is Tahoe Tessie," *Reno News & Review*, January 22, 2004.

Rocha, Guy Louis. "Getting to the Bottom of Lake Tahoe," Myth #151, Nevada Historical Myth of the Month, www.nevadaculture.org.

Sheffield, Keith. "Dark Shapes in the Lake: Tahoe Tessie Remains Alive for Visitors," *Tahoe Tribune*, April 29, 2005.

Stienstra, Tom. "Mysteries of the Deep at Lake Tahoe," *San Francisco Chronicle*, July 25, 2004.

LOVELOCK'S REDHEADED GIANTS

Brooks, Sheilagh, Carolyn Stark, and Richard H. Brooks. "John Reid's Redheaded 'Giants' of Central Nevada: Fact or Fiction?" *Nevada Historic Society Quarterly*, Winter 1984.

Dansie, Dorothy P. "John T. Reid's Case for the Redheaded Giants," *Nevada Historic Society Quarterly*, Fall 1975.

"Fossil Find Upsets Scientific Theory," *New York Times*, March 9, 1924.

Lovelock Review-Miner, June 19, 1931.

"Mystery of the Petrified Shoe Sole," *New York Sunday American*, March 19, 1922.

Winnemucca, Sarah. *Life Among the Paiutes: Their Wrongs and Claims*. Reno, NV: University of Nevada Press, 1883.

Pyramid Lake's Water Babies and Other Spirits

Benson, Larry. "The Tufas of Pyramid Lake, Nevada," US Geological Survey, www.plpt.nsn.us/geology/index.html.

Francaviglia, Richard V. *Believing in Place: A Spiritual Geography of the Great Basin*. Reno, NV: University of Nevada Press, 2003.

NUMA: A Northern Paiute History. Sparks, NV: The Inter-Tribal Council of Nevada, 1976.

The Garden of Eden in Nevada

Chalekian, Harry A. "Was the Garden of Eden Located in Nevada?" *Nevada Magazine*, July–August 1993.

Fox, William L. *The Void, the Grid & the Sign*. Reno, NV: University of Nevada Press, 2005.

Francaviglia, Richard V. *Believing in Place: A Spiritual Geography of the Great Basin*. Reno, NV: University of Nevada Press, 2003.

San Francisco Examiner, August 17, 1924.

———. August 18, 1924.

———. August 19, 1924.

Theosophy magazine, April 1925.

Haunted Carson City

"Carson City Ghostwalk, 2005," http://aroundcarson.com/carsoncity/ghostwalk2005.html.

"Ghosts of Carson City," http://computer-vet.com/travel/carson/ghosts.html.

Hauck, Dennis William. *The National Directory of Haunted Places*. New York: Penquin Books, 1994.

"Haunted Laxalt: Carson City, Nevada's Most Haunted Building," http://hauntedlaxalt.blogspot.com/.

"Nevada's Haunted Hotspots," www.carpenoctem.tv/haunt/nv.

Oberding, Jane. *Haunted Nevada*. Boca Raton, FL: Universal Publishers, 2001. www.hauntednevada.com/hauntedplaces.html.

Pryor, Alton. *The Bawdy House Girls: A Look at the Brothels of the Old West*. Roseville, CA: Stagecoach Publishing, 2006.

THE GREAT CARSON CITY STAGECOACH ROBBERY

Atwater, Jane. "Lost Wells Fargo Gold," *Desert Magazine*, 1954.

Coin World magazine website, www.coinworld.com.

Conrotto, Eugene L. *Lost Gold and Silver Mines of the Southwest*. Mineola, NY: Dover Publications, 1996.

Earl, Philip I. "Confidence Man," *Nevada Magazine*, September–October 2005.

Paher, Stanley W. *Nevada: An Annotated Bibliography*. Las Vegas: Nevada Publications, 1980.

Penrose, Matt, and John K. Meredith. *Pots O' Gold*. Reno, NV: A. Carlisle & Co, 1935.

Rocha, Guy Louis. "What Didn't Happen in Carson City," Myth #131, Nevada Historical Myth of the Month, www.nevadaculture.org.

THE FIRST TRAIN ROBBERY IN THE FAR WEST

Central Pacific Railroad Photographic History Museum, http://cprr.org/Museum/Robbery.html.

Kinkead, James H. "The First Train Robbery on the Pacific Coast," The Third Biennial Report of the Nevada Historical Society, 1913.

Lingenfelter, Richard E. *Death Valley & the Amargosa: A Land of Illusion.* Berkeley, CA: University of California Press, 1986.

"Reno Turns 100," *Reno News and Review*, March 20, 2003.

"Robbed Twice on the Same Day," Howard Hickson's Histories, www.outbacknv.us/howh/CPRR.html.

Rocha, Guy Louis. "The Verdi Train Robbery Didn't Happen in Verdi," Myth #55, Nevada Historical Myth of the Month, www.nevadaculture.org.

Wilson, R. Michael. *Great Train Robberies of the Old West.* Guilford, CT: TwoDot, 2006.

THE MYSTERY OF THE LOST CITY

Harrington, M.R. *Ancient Tribes of the Boulder Dam Country.* Los Angeles: Southwest Museum, 1937.

Higginbotham, Leslie. "Lost City Discovered in Nevada Sands: Ruins Near Muddy River Give Evidence of a Cultured and Intelligent People," *New York Times*, February 8, 1925.

Hopkins, A. D., and K. J. Evans. *The First 100: Portraits of the Men and Women Who Shaped Las Vegas*. Las Vegas: Huntington Press, 2000.

Lost City Museum History, www.comnett.net/~lostcity/LCM2.htm.

"Science: The Diggers," *Time* magazine, April 26, 1926.

Scrugham, James G. *Nevada: The Narrative of the Conquest of a Frontier Land*. Chicago: American History Society, 1935.

THE FIRST NATIONAL BANK OF WINNEMUCCA ROBBERY

Meadows, Anne. *Digging Up Butch and Sundance*. Lincoln, NE: Bison Books, 2003.

Rocha, Guy Louis. "The Wild Bunch in Winnemucca," Myth #92, Nevada Historical Myth of the Month, www.nevadaculture.org.

Toll, David W. "Butch Cassidy and the Great Winnemucca Bank Robbery," *Nevada Magazine*, May–June 1983.

THE UNKNOWN FATE OF ROY FRISCH

"Baby Face" Nelson, FBI History, www.fbi.gov/libref/historic/famcases/babyface/babyface.htm.

Raymond, C. Elizabeth. "George Wingfield: Owner and Operator of Nevada," Reno, NV: University of Nevada Press, 1992.

"Reno Crime 'Bosses' Found Guilty Here," *New York Times*, February 13, 1938.

"Reno Is Unruffled by Gamblers' Fall," *New York Times*, February 20, 1938.

"Report Missing Banker Slain at Reno by Nelson," *Chicago Daily Tribune*, July 14, 1935.

Toll, David W. "Finding Roy Frisch," www.nevadatravel.net/travelgram/07-07.html.

AREA 51: THE TRUTH IS OUT THERE

"Area 51," www.answers.com.

"In the Nevada desert, there's something out there—the Black Mailbox," *Los Angeles Times*, August 21, 2008.

"Little A'Le'Inn," www.littlealeinn.com.

Patton, Phil. *Dreamland*. New York: Villard, 1998.

Strickland, Jonathan. "How Area 51 Works," www.science.how stuffworks.com.

"Unsolved History: Area 51," Discovery Channel, February 17, 2005.

WHY DID GANGSTER BUGSY SIEGEL DIE?

"Bugsy Siegel and the Flamingo Hotel," Online Nevada Encyclopedia, www.onlinenevada.org./bugsy_siegel_and_the _flamingo_hotel.

Gribben, Mark. *"Bugsy Siegel,"* www.dark-horse.co.uk/gangsters/
bugsy/bugsymain.htm.

Hopkins, A. D., and K. J. Evans. *The First 100: Portraits of
the Men and Women Who Shaped Las Vegas*. Las Vegas:
Huntington Press, 2000.

"Mob Ties," *Las Vegas Sun*, May 15, 2008.

Sheehan, Jack, ed. *The Players: The Men Who Made Las Vegas*.
Reno, NV: University of Nevada Press, 1997.

"Siegel, Gangster Is Slain on Coast," *New York Times,* June 22,
1947.

Smith, John L. "In Search of Bugsy Siegel," *Nevada Magazine,*
May–June 1994.

Wilkerson, W.R., III. *The Man Who Invented Las Vegas*.
Bellingham, WA: Ciro's Books, 2000.

WALKER LAKE'S SEA SERPENTS

Johnson, Edward. *Walker River Paiute History*. Walker River Tribe
Publications, 1975.

Numa: A Northern Paiute History. Sparks, NV: The Inter-Tribal
Council of Nevada, 1976.

Walker Lake Interpretive Association, www.walkerlakenv.org

Washington Herald (Indiana), September 22, 1907.

Wheeler, Sessions S. *The Desert Lake: The Story of Nevada's
Pyramid Lake*. Caldwell, ID: Caxton Press, 2001.

THE CONQUEROR'S CURSE

Adams, Cecil. Straight Dope, *Chicago Reader*, October 26, 1984.

Jackovich, Karen G., and Mark Sennet, "The Children of John Wayne, Susan Hayward, and Dick Powell Fear That Fallout Killed Their Parents," *People Magazine,* November 10, 1980.

Roberts, Randy, and James Stuart Olson. *John Wayne: American.* Lincoln, NE: Bison Books, 1997.

Seegmiller, Janet Burton. *The History of Iron County; Nuclear Testing and the Downwinders.* http://historytogo.utah.gov/utah _chapters/utah_today/nucleartestingandthedownwinders.html.

THE STRANGE DEATH OF ADVENTURER STEVE FOSSETT

Ayres, Chris. "Facts Ruin Otherwise Good Steve Fossett Conspiracy Theories," *The Times,* October 3, 2008.

Chong, Jia-Rui, and Steve Chawkins. "Fossett's Widow Thanks Hiker," *Los Angeles Times*, October 3, 2008.

Cone, Tracie, and Juliana Barbassa, "Fossett Searchers Pursue Debris," *Las Vegas Review-Journal*, October 3, 2008.

———. "Missing Adventurer: Wreckage, Bone Found at Crash Site," *Las Vegas Review-Journal*, October 3, 2008.

Dittrich, Luke. "What I Learned Looking for Steve Fossett," *Esquire* magazine, June 2008.

"DNA Links Bones Near Plane Crash Site to Fossett," *Associated Press*, November 3, 2008.

"Fossett Plane Recovery Might Not Resume this Year," *Reno Gazette-Journal*, October 5, 2008.

"Hope Fades in Search for Fossett," *New York Times*, September 7, 2007.

Irvine, Chris. "Adventurer Steve Fossett 'may have faked his own death,'" *The Telegraph,* July 28, 2008.

Merrill, Jamie. "Into Thin Air: Did Steve Fossett Fake His Own Death?" *The Independent,* August 1, 2008.

Nieves, Evelyn and Scott Sonner. "Mystery Enshrouds Fossett's Final Flight," *Reno Gazette-Journal*, October 5, 2008.

"Steve Fossett Officially Dead, But Hope Still Lingers," *Nevada Appeal,* February 17, 2008.

Vlahos, James. "Steve Fossett Special Report: The Vanishing," *National Geographic Adventure*, December 2007.

Vogel, Ed. "Costly Search Was Off Target," *Las Vegas Review-Journal,* October 2, 2008.

WHO SHOT RENO CASINO OWNER LINCOLN FITZGERALD?

Hagar, Ray. "Fitzgeralds Closes, 474 Laid Off, Will Reopen After Renovations," *Reno Gazette-Journal*, September 30, 2008.

"History of the Nevada Club," www.oldreno.net.

Kefauver Crime Committee Reports, Testimony of Virgil W. Peterson, 1951.

Kling, Dwayne. *The Rise of the Biggest Little City: An Encyclopedic History of Reno Gaming, 1931–1981*. Reno, NV: University of Nevada Press, 1999.

"Reno Gambler Shot by Assassin at Home," *Pittsburgh Post-Gazette*, November 20, 1949.

"Reno Gambling Club Operator Shot in Ambush," *St. Petersburg Times*, November 20, 1949.

Riley, Dylan. "Michigan Native Lincoln Fitzgerald Is Attacked by Unknown Assailant," *Reno News and Review*, March 20, 2003.

"Shotgun Ambush Cuts Down Nevada Gambler," *Evening Independent* (St. Petersburg, FL), November 19, 1949.

WHY DID THRIVING METROPOLIS TURN INTO A GHOST TOWN?

"Have You Purchased a Lot at Metropolis, Nevada?" Nevada State Journal, April 17, 1912.

"Look Into Metropolis, Nevada," The Salt Lake Tribune, September 1, 1911.

"Metropolis Ghosts Are Skeptics About Oil After the Great Downfall of Early Plans," Nevada State Journal, February 28, 1954.

"New Line Taps Reclaimed Area," San Francisco Call, January 26, 1912.

"An Opportunity for Every Man at Metropolis, Nevada," Goodwin's Weekly, Salt Lake City, August 19, 1911.

SUICIDE OR SOMETHING ELSE?
THE MYSTERIOUS DEATH OF RAYMOND SPILSBURY

"Body of Raymond Spilsbury Found," *Iron County Record*, March 1, 1945.

"Clues Are Missing on Lost Fisherman," *The Arizona Republic*, February 25, 1945.

"Ex-Mining Official Believed River Victim," *The Courier-Journal* (Louisville, KY), January 24, 1945.

"Filing Shows $237,313 Left by Nevadan," The Salt Lake Tribune, May 12, 1945.

"Inquest Scheduled in Copper Man's Death," The Los Angeles Times, March 1, 1945.

"Man Is Missing on Colorado River," *The Reno Gazette*, January 24, 1945

McBride, Dennis. Midnight on Arizona Street: The Secret Life of the Boulder Dam Hotel. Boulder City, NV: Boulder City/Hoover Dam Museum, 1993.

Metallurgy Magazine, American Institute of Mining and Metallurgical Engineers, 1911.

"Mine Operator's Body Found," *The Montana Standard*, February 27, 1945.

"Mining Man's Body Found Shackled, *The Salt Lake Tribune*, February 28, 1945.

"Murder, He Writes," *Las Vegas Sun*, October 10, 1996.

"Raymond Spilsbury's Body Found in Colorado," Washington County News, March 3, 1945.

"Spilsbury Found; Thought Suicide," Nevada State Journal, March 1, 1945.

"Utahn Returns from Peru Stay," *The Sunday Herald* (Provo, UT), December 3, 1944.

Wood, Robert S. Desert Riverman: The Free-Spirited Adventures of Murl Emery. Flagstaff, AZ: Fretwater Press, 2009.

INDEX

Richard Moreno is the author of ten Nevada-related books, including *Nevada Curiosities* (Globe Pequot) and *A Short History of Reno, Second Edition* (University of Nevada Press). He served as publisher of *Nevada Magazine* for fourteen years and was honored with the Nevada Writers Hall of Fame Silver Pen Award in 2007. He currently works as Director of Content Development at Central Washington University. He resides in Ellensburg, Washington, with his wife, but makes regular visits to the Silver State.

Printed in the USA
CPSIA information can be obtained
at www.ICGtesting.com
LVHW040907100324
774066LV00005B/160